FOCUS ON THE FAM

C000274789

TONY EVANS
KINGDOM SINGLE

LIVING COMPLETE
AND FULLY FREE

TYNDALE

Tyndale House Publishers, Inc.
Carol Stream, Illinois

Kingdom Single: Living Complete and Fully Free

A Focus on the Family book published by Tyndale House Publishers, Inc., Carol Stream, Illinois 60188

Focus on the Family and the accompanying logo and design are federally registered trademarks of Focus on the Family, 8605 Explorer Drive, Colorado Springs, CO 80920.

TYNDALE and Tyndale's quill logo are registered trademarks of Tyndale House Publishers, Inc.

People's names and certain details of their stories have been changed to protect the privacy of the individuals involved. However, the facts of what happened and the underlying principles have been conveyed as accurately as possible.

Cover design by Sally Dunn
Cover photo by Sally Dunn

For information about special discounts for bulk purchases, please contact Tyndale House Publishers at csresponse@tyndale.com, or call 1-800-323-9400.

ISBN 978-1-58997-951-2 (HC)
ISBN 978-1-58997-669-6 (SC)

Printed in the United States of America

25   24   23   22   21   20   19
7   6   5   4   3   2   1

This book is lovingly dedicated to my sisters-in-law—Ruth Ann Cannings, Bernice Cannings, and Elizabeth Cannings—and to my special niece Clarise, for their conscientious review and input on this book. Thank you for your investment in my life, my ministry, and my family.

CONTENTS

PART I

THE CONCEPT
OF A
KINGDOM
SINGLE

1

THE COMPLETENESS OF SINGLES

An omelet is only as good as the eggs you put into it.

That's probably not how you expected a book on singleness to begin, but stick with me for a moment. When you cook an omelet and you crack open two rotten eggs, you will wind up with a nasty-tasting omelet. Even if one egg is good and the other egg is rotten, you will still wind up with a nasty-tasting omelet. The good egg is not going to make the bad egg better. No, the bad egg is going to contaminate the good egg.

Simply put: One bad egg destroys a good egg and causes the omelet to become inedible.

What does cooking an omelet have to do with singleness?

Everything.

Far too often, the discussions surrounding the topic of being single focus primarily on the future aspect of finding a mate. They focus on how to "wait well" until the joining together of the two "eggs" creates a marriage. In fact, most singles I talk to, counsel, or pastor are so keyed in on finding their future spouse, praying for marriage, or looking for a romantic partner that they altogether miss the benefits, purposes, and importance of singleness. They miss the critical aspects of cultivating a healthy life themselves while also setting their standards high enough for their future spouse. When the benefits, purposes, and importance of singleness are skipped in a person's developmental process, you wind up with a rotten marriage later on.

Thus, my goal in this book is not to advise you on how to wait well. No, my desire is to completely shift your thinking out of the waiting cycle. This is because, from my experience in counseling hundreds of singles over the years, emphasizing a "waiting well" mentality leads to a multiplicity of unintended—but very real—consequences.

To encourage someone to live in a posture of waiting for something or someone places that person in a perpetual state of conscious want, need, and future-oriented thinking. It produces a mentality of lack. In thinking that way, the individual runs the risk of missing out on the *now*.

If this describes *you*, you run the risk of selling yourself short during your present. You run the risk of settling for less than the best in a rush to make the future happen sooner than it ought. You run the risk of exchanging a life you passionately embrace one day at a time for a life where you simply exist as you look for the next part to come along. And that is not what I want for you.

That's not what God wants for you.

Kingdom single, you are not merely to learn how to wait well.

Now, don't close these pages fearing what I might say next. I'm not going to walk you down the all-too-familiar path for singles, telling you that "God is your husband" and that this truth should be enough. I understand singleness is not a permanent calling for most people. In fact, most surveys reveal that roughly 90 percent of all singles *want* to get married. Singleness is not some super-spiritual status chosen by everyone. I realize that many people are single due to the breakdown in our culture and a dismissal of family values. Divorce, selfishness, a consumerist mind-set, and overall relational dysfunction in families of origin and social circles have led to a cultural shift that has delayed the onset of marriage and availability of healthy (mentally and spiritually), stable marital options.

Yes, God is your husband (Isaiah 54:5), but that doesn't mean He brings you flowers, opens your car door, fixes your garbage disposal, keeps your feet warm at night, helps you find your contact lens when you drop it, or gives you hugs when you feel vulnerable and alone. To say that God is your husband from a spiritual standpoint is true. But to say you have no remaining physical or emotional needs, whether as a man or a woman, is naïve.

Living as a successful, satisfied single ... comes in learning how to walk that tightrope of waiting for the future yet also fully embracing the present, or longing for more yet still delighting if more simply never arrives.

One of my closest friends over the course of my life started out as my professor and mentor. His name was Zane Hodges. Zane passed away at the full age of seventy-six after decades of service to God as a seminary professor, Bible scholar, pastor, and author. Zane loved his work and dedicated his life to it and to the people he shepherded. Zane was also never married.

I'll never forget the somber, quiet tone he used one day in the latter years of his life when he told me: "Tony, there is a loss that comes with being single. With all the spiritual goodness and profits that surround it, there is this reality of a deep loss when you're single. It is a space that isn't filled; there is something you feel that is missing because there are physical and relational needs that are just not met."

Zane's words struck me with sadness. But then he continued, "That loss, though, does not have to negate your being content."

That's the dichotomy. There are chasms that exist in singleness that can't simply be wished away or filled with ice cream, activities, shopping, addictions, or even church attendance. There is a polarity that produces real, felt struggles. Living as a successful, satisfied single will not come without intentionality. But it can come. It comes in learning how to walk that tightrope of waiting for the future yet also fully embracing the present, or longing for more yet still delighting if more simply never arrives.

It's not easy to do, I'm sure. And this won't be an easy book to read. It certainly hasn't been easy to write. Keep in mind that everyone is different, and some things I say may or may not apply to you. God's plans for people's lives are as varied as the wildflowers in a field. That being so, some things may hit you closer to home than others, while other things may hit someone else closer to home. Yet the overarching general principles threaded throughout ought to provide a framework upon which stability, strength, and satisfaction can be woven into the unique tapestry of your own life.

Show Me the Marriage

Let me return to the subject of eggs.

In the 1999 hit movie *Runaway Bride*, Maggie Carpenter (played by Julia Roberts) struggled with making it all the way to the altar. Engaged multiple times, she would break off an engagement shortly before (or even on) the wedding day. The movie looked at the different reasons this might have happened to her, arriving at the conclusion that Maggie simply didn't know how she liked her own eggs prepared.

Of course, that's a simplistic explanation to a deep issue, but the bottom line was that Maggie found herself acquiescing to the likes, preferences, and desires of each man she became engaged to, all the while never quite knowing her own. When asked one day how she wanted her eggs cooked, she didn't have an answer.

In short, she didn't know her own passions, skills, dreams, and preferences because she was so focused on one day fulfilling the dream (and pressure) of being a wife. It wasn't until Maggie identified who *she* was and truly became *Maggie* that she was able to marry.

This film's story line actually goes against the norm of how most movies portray the romantic relationship. Moving away from eggs and omelets and over to football and sports agents, we find the more typical scene displayed in the box-office hit *Jerry Maguire*.

If you're like most Americans, you probably know by heart the scene I'm about to describe. Tom Cruise's character stands in a room full of women, seated comfortably on couches and chairs, as he interrupts their book club evening with his emotional expression of love. As tears threaten to wet his cheeks, he says to his love interest (played by Renee Zellweger) standing across the room, "We live in a cynical world, and we work in a business of tough competitors." He then pauses as the room draws and holds a collective breath. He continues: "I love you. You . . . complete . . . me."

Starting to say something else, he is quickly interrupted by Renee's character, who softly and sweetly replies, "Shut up. Just shut up. You had me at hello."

The two characters then make their way toward each other as the music builds and they become locked in each other's arms. The supporting cast cries and sniffs on cue, the romantic couple are now one, and countless millions of people absorb a distorted view of singleness and romantic relationships while applauding all the same.

This scene and its message (not the takeaway principle in *Runaway Bride*) is the overarching theme of relationships in modern media. It appears over and over again, whether in movies, songs, talk shows, or articles. This theme spells out the purported purpose of romance and marriage, according to popular culture. Which makes it no big surprise that far too many people continue living in perpetual wait-mode—waiting for the *Jerry Maguire* moment of finding that special someone to whom they can finally say, "You complete me."

But that statement is fundamentally wrong. It is also fiercely frightening, because when one incomplete person marries another incomplete person, you wind up with two incomplete people living together in what most often results in a hot mess. Don't lose your pursuit of completeness because of your desire to be married.

> *A kingdom single may want to be married, but the difference is that he or she doesn't need to be married to feel complete and whole.*

If you are not yet complete, please don't get married.

Many unmarried people are looking for marriage to achieve something it cannot do, namely fix their broken and incomplete selves. Often that means getting attached to another broken and incomplete unmarried person, creating defective and unfulfilling relationships. A kingdom single may want to be married, but the difference is that he or she doesn't need to be married to feel complete and whole. If you need to be married, you have not yet fully understood or embraced your status as a kingdom single.

Far too many couples are married and yet still feel alone because they never fully knew what it meant to be fully single. So they are grasping for something both in and from their spouse that their spouse often lacks the capacity to provide. The nature of marriage is not merely what you're *getting from* someone else, but also what you're *giving to* someone else. And what you should be giving your spouse is a completely whole single Christian, not half of one who is incomplete.

Friend, you are not fully ready to be married until you're a fully functioning kingdom single. Otherwise, like most people, all you're doing is bringing your incompleteness into a relationship, expecting that relationship to accomplish what it is unable to do. All the marriage will do is reveal that you never fully learned what it meant to be single. To put it succinctly, you are complete in Christ with or without marriage.

If you're looking for a romantic partner to complete you as a kingdom single, you really don't understand what Jesus Christ has already done. Because in Him, you are as complete as complete comes. Now, you may not realize that truth. You may not identify with that truth. And if you don't, you're not living out the full benefits of that truth. But none of those things makes the truth any less true. Colossians 2:10 tells us, "In Him you have been made complete, and He is the head over all rule and authority." To think otherwise is to make the institution of marriage, and your desire for a marriage partner, an idol. And idolatry is sin.

Friend, Jesus Christ completes you. That's the truth. Thus, what a romantic partner can provide must remain outside of that, in addition to it, or alongside it. He or she cannot complete you, because Jesus already has. If you are not aware or mindful of this reality, there's a danger that you will be expecting too much of another human being, asking him or her to be or do something that only God Himself can be and do.

Far too often, we try to transfer what we see in movies to our real lives. But that places pressure on us and the other people in our lives to live up to a standard we were never designed to fulfill.

As you grow in your understanding, discovery, and acceptance of your completeness in Jesus Christ, you will experience the victory, authority, and intimacy He has already secured for you in Him. You will then be freed up to experience other relationships at a level they were designed for.

When God created Eve so that Adam would not be "alone" (Genesis 2:18), the word used to describe what He gave to Adam was a "helper" (Hebrew: *ezer*, meaning "a strong help") who was "suitable" (Hebrew: *neged*, meaning "before, about, behind, in the presence of"). Eve wasn't created because Adam lacked anything in and of himself. In fact, Adam had to give up a part of himself in the process of gaining Eve. Nor was Eve designed to complete something missing within Adam, or even within herself. Rather, she was created to come alongside him (and he alongside her) in this thing called life in order to fulfill a kingdom assignment. And just as the word *neged* indicates, sometimes that would mean "before," while other times it may mean "behind," and still others simply "in the presence or proximity of."

Relational issues arise when the focus of either person (or both) shifts from God to each other as the deciding factor, influencer, or even source of completion. That's exactly what happened in the Garden of Eden, after all, which led to the Fall.

Only when you understand and embrace the truth that Christ Himself completes you will you be able to view any current or potential relationship for what it can actually provide—a companion to come alongside you. You'll be amazed at how fulfilling and satisfying a relationship can be when expectations are normalized, the benefit of the doubt (coupled with grace) becomes natural, and you both look to God to lead, fill, satisfy, and complete you.

Imagine the strain and drain a relationship suffers when one or both people look to the other as their source of completion. Modern psychiatry might call that codependency, not love. Keep in mind, no human being is equipped to offer you what it cost the God of the universe—His own Son's life—to both win and secure. So the first step in living with a kingdom mind-set is understanding that by Christ's sitting next to the Father on the throne, Christ has declared both His ability and His right to complete you.

What does it mean to live as a complete single?

Our English word *single* comes from the joining of the Latin word *singulus* and the Old French word *simplus*. Together, they become more than what most people understand the cultural, contemporary term *single* to mean. Rather than "alone," "unattached," "unmarried," or "by oneself," a more literal translation of these two original words would be "simply unique" or "uniquely simple." Both of those better illustrate the biblical concept of singleness. Other defining terms attached to the original words are "singular," "complete," and "whole."

God never established singleness to be a burdensome, lonesome, pointless, and frustrating existence, as so many have falsely labeled it today. Rather, it is the very "simplicity" of the single life (which we will go into more deeply in Scripture later) that frees a person to fully live out his or her own "uniqueness" and "completeness."

Singleness positions people to become their best version of themselves as no other relational role can. God does not want singles to look to marriage as a way to stop being *single*. People are always to maintain their wholeness, completeness, and uniqueness as individuals, even (and especially) when they get married.

Unfortunately, that is rarely what's communicated to Christian singles today, either verbally or nonverbally. The church is largely at fault for making singles feel like second-class and incomplete citizens, as most of the events, activities, small groups, and formal messages focus primarily on married couples and families, with little or no application for singles. Yet singles make up roughly half of our entire American adult population. Any way you slice it, nearly half of an entire country is a huge portion of the country. The statistics in the church are similar, if not even more slanted toward singles.

> *Singleness positions people to become their best version of themselves as no other relational role can.*

With such a great number of singles in America and in the church, why is so little said on the subject from the pulpit? I'll conjecture that it may have something to do with the fact that nearly every senior pastor is married. And if a pastor becomes divorced at some point in his career, he will typically resign from the ministry. Thus, you have an entire layer of spiritual leadership living in the context of marriage while overseeing the development of half (if not more) of their congregation in an entirely different context.

I can say from firsthand experience that a pastor who happens to be married is always on dangerous ground when he approaches the issue of singleness. Invariably he hears the accusation, "Pastor, you don't understand. You've been married for so long. You don't know the struggles I face as a single!" I've heard this myself more times than I care to remember.

And it's natural for people to feel that a married pastor cannot relate to them because he hasn't experienced what they're experiencing. However, the truth of the Word transcends our experiences. I have never been an alcoholic, for example, but I can tell you what the Bible has to say about it. I can speak because God has spoken. I have never struggled with fear or anxiety, but I can deliver other people from it. I've been married for more than forty-five years, yes, but I also know what God says about singleness and the topics that directly correlate to it. Add to that decades of counseling singles and I feel prepared to teach on this subject in a way that is compassionate, understanding, empowering, and empathetic. Not only was I single before I got married, but I've also taken the time to listen to those who are, or have been, and I've thoroughly studied God's Word on the subject.

Nevertheless, I understand the need of many of you to hear from someone who knows firsthand what the single lifestyle is really like. That's why I've chosen to borrow heavily from the words of someone who was single for a long time. I'm talking about the apostle Paul.

The apostle Paul personally understood the strengths and successes of the single lifestyle far better than do the social commentators of our day. His inspired words in the New Testament present us with a challenge that cuts across the grain of our society. According to Paul:

Being single is a very good thing (see 1 Corinthians 7:26).

Yes, there's a good deal of controversy surrounding that concept, even though it's every bit as biblical as John 3:16. But make no mistake about what Paul is saying: *If you are single, you're in the best possible spiritual position.*

Now, this may be contrary to what you've heard about singleness or even what you feel about it, but God's Word often runs contrary to popular opinion. God never set out to be popular. He set out to be God. And God says it is highly beneficial for a person to be single. God is not opposed to marriage; He created it, and it has its own purposes. But when comparing the two for which state allows for the understanding and fulfilling of one's purpose, being single wins.

Whether you want to be single or married, let that truth sink in for a moment. Let the high value God places on your status assure you that your life is not a mistake and this season does not have to be disappointing.

Singleness is not a second-class status. It's not to be a perpetual waiting period. Singleness is a unique platform and position provided to you for great enjoyment, accomplishment, discovery, exploration, freedom, and meaning. To not maximize your season of singleness because you're so focused on waiting for marriage or disappointed in the present is to waste your God-given gift. Never miss out on today's open doors for those you are hoping will open tomorrow.

Never miss out on today's open doors for those you are hoping will open tomorrow.

It Started with a Single

God did not create Adam and Eve as a married couple. Rather, they were created as adult singles first. In fact, the first single person God created was a man. Far too often in the church, we hear that all the messages and events on singleness are aimed at women. But when the Bible is our source of learning, we see numerous examples of God's using single men as models for how kingdom singles should live. Jesus, Daniel, Joseph, Paul, Isaac, and the three Hebrew men in the furnace are good examples. However, the principles of singleness in these pages transcend gender, whether the person from whose life we derive a standard is male or female.

From the beginning of time, though, God initiated singleness by first creating a man. What we learn from this example is that God gave Adam a personal relationship with Him first. He gave him a calling and His instruction prior to giving him a mate. Every single man, in particular, should thus prioritize these areas during his time of singleness, so that if and when it's time to get married, he can offer his future bride a kingdom man.

Genesis 2:18 gives us our first look at what it means to fully live as a unique, complete single. We read, "Then the LORD God said, 'It is not good for the man to be alone; I will make him a helper suitable for him.'" We often misread that verse, assuming God is saying that it's not good for man to be single. But He doesn't say that. He says it's not good for man to be *alone*. There's a difference. When you look at this concept, you must distinguish between being single and being alone and not equate the two.

On the dresser as I write this chapter is my key ring. On my key ring are two different keys. One is round and one is oblong. One key goes to a door at home, while the other is a master key for the doors at church. Each key has been created with indentations and protrusions sufficient to unlock the door it was designed to unlock.

To use each key does not require the help of the other key. Each key functions wholly on its own. In other words, these two different keys are completely independent of each other.

Yet as I mentioned, I also have a key ring. And while both keys function independently of each other, they are both likewise connected to each other through a ring. Putting keys on a ring doesn't change the nature of the keys. The keys remain as they were before without the ring because they were already complete. All the ring did was hook up two complete keys so that they could now remain connected in the same vicinity.

Friend, if you don't view yourself as already complete as a single, then you will function as an incomplete single and thus be subject to illegitimate bondage because you have a wrong perception of yourself. God said it is not good that man should be alone. Not that it is not good that man is single.

Under God's rule in the Garden, singleness meant to be complete, whole, and unique. This is why God was the one who determined Adam was alone. Adam was not initially aware of any concept of aloneness. That's because until God told him, he wasn't alone. Likewise, God doesn't want you to equate being single with being alone. God wanted Adam to be completely fulfilled in Him before He gave him a mate. A mate became a bonus.

> *God did not begin humanity with a married couple. He began with two singles.*

Likewise, when God created Eve as a single adult woman, she didn't open her eyes and shriek, "Oh, no, I'm single! What's going to become of me?" Rather, God had to bring her to Adam. Before that happened, she was already complete in who she was.

God did not begin humanity with a married couple. He began with two singles. And remember, Adam got his mate while he was sleeping, not panicking.

In fact, Adam had even been given a crucial, divine assignment to fulfill before he was provided with a "helper." Genesis 2:15 says, "Then the LORD God took the man and put him into the garden of Eden to cultivate it and keep it." God also assigned him to name the animals in it (Genesis 2:19, 20a). Thus, before Adam ever became attached to Eve, he was called upon to maximize his full potential by turning the Garden into an organized, productive place.

This means that the key to your completeness as a single is rooted first and foremost in your calling, not your sexuality. Because Adam was so busy as a kingdom single doing kingdom work, God had to tell him he needed a helper. Likewise, as you're busy fulfilling your kingdom role and purpose, you should be fully content until God changes your status, or even if He doesn't.

Before there was an Eve, Adam utilized his intellectual capacity in naming the animals. Not only that, but whatever he chose to name an animal, God backed him on it. God supported and blessed Adam's work as a single. Thus, Adam truly was a *kingdom* single. A kingdom single is defined as *an unmarried Christian who is committed to fully and freely maximizing his or her completeness under the rule of God and the lordship of Jesus Christ.*

Which leads us to the question on the floor: What made Adam a kingdom single so that he could fully and freely live out his completeness under God? A few principles come out of his story that can help answer that question. First, Adam possessed a clearly defined divine identity. Genesis 1:26 says, "Then God said, 'Let Us make man in Our image, according to Our likeness.'"

Likewise, every man and every woman possesses this image of God, because we are all made in His image. You have a divine stamp on your soul, which means your identity is to be rooted first and foremost in your relationship with the One in whose image you're made. You are never to define yourself by a relationship to someone else, because when you're defined by another person, you have created a competing image to God. Not only is that image competing, but it's also corrupt. What makes you a unique and special single is that you're created in the image of God. Your connection to God and not another person should give you your ultimate sense of worth and significance.

One of my most difficult jobs as a pastor is to get people to understand that their ultimate commitment is to God, not people. Your identity is in God, not in others. It's not even in what you do. The Bible condemns idolatry in numerous places, but rarely do we, in our Western mind-sets, consider another person to be an idol. Yet an idol is any person, place, or thing that you look to above or in place of God's rightful position in your time, talents, thoughts, and choices. If you're looking to another person as your identity, meaning, purpose, or source, you have an idol—even if that other person is a future mate you haven't even met yet.

You were uniquely and specifically created to mirror the identity of the Creator Himself. He is your source, purpose, meaning, and identity. That being so, no human being and nothing else can ever possibly complete you. You are complete as you are. You are whole, made in the image of God Himself.

One of the first things that will help you mentally to embrace your wholeness is to begin to define yourself as God defines you. Don't let the devil carry out identity theft on your singleness. Nothing else can define you. Not what your mom said, nor your dad, nor even what has been done to you or you have done yourself. You can be defined only by your identity with God, which means you are a blood-bought child of the King, with royalty flowing through your veins. You are an heir to the kingdom, with a purpose that extends beyond yourself. You are whole. You are unique. You are complete.

Another principle that comes from Adam's story is that he was given divine instruction to freely eat of the trees of the garden. Far too often, we focus on the one tree Adam was instructed to avoid. But Genesis 2:16 says, "The LORD God commanded the man, saying, 'From any tree of the garden you may eat freely.'" This was an instruction to a single man. And it wasn't a suggestion; it was a command. God commanded Adam, meaning Adam was supposed to do this. It wasn't up for discussion or negotiation. If he were to operate under the Lord God, that would be how he was to roll. He was commanded to freely eat and enjoy all that was available to him.

That's a lot of freedom. I define biblical freedom as *the release from illegitimate bondage so that you can make the choice to maximize your potential.* Adam had the entire known world open to him for enjoyment, barring one tree. Yes, there was that one restriction, but his freedom was a lot bigger than the restriction. In fact, the first command ever given to humanity was (to put it in everyday language), "Enjoy yourself." Why? Because a kingdom single is free—free to maximize the potential of the gift of life itself.

Friend, from a biblical standpoint, you should be living it up as a single. Adam was supposed to be living it up as a single. He was supposed to be spending so much time having fun in the garden, because there was so much given to him that he was commanded to freely enjoy.

Being all you were created to be and fully living your life is a command. You'd better enjoy yourself. You'd better express yourself. You'd better be all you can be, because it's a command. So if you're a boring, stuck-at-home, not-enjoying-life single, you're disobeying God—literally disobeying Him and setting yourself up for temptation on the one tree you're not supposed to mess with.

> *So if you're a boring, stuck-at-home, not-enjoying-life single, you're disobeying God.*

The purpose of the restriction was crucial to Adam's maximizing his completeness as a kingdom single. It was a perpetual reminder that he was not autonomous. He was not to determine good and evil or right and wrong independently of God. Only with the restriction could he enjoy and maximize the massive amount of freedom God made available to him.

Likewise, God restricts us in order to liberate us. Just as the boundary lines on a tennis court are there to provide a framework within which to play, God's boundaries give us the ability to fully and freely maximize our lives. Without the boundaries on a tennis court, there could be no game. Without the sidelines on a football field, there would be chaos.

Rather than view God's boundaries as a negative, therefore, seek to see what they actually provide—the ability to enjoy all He has provided within a context of peace and order. You have been given the opportunity to fully and freely live all your life to its highest potential and enjoyment as a single. To not do so is to belittle God's gift of life. Yes, there are boundaries as a single, but when you shift your eyes from the boundaries to the playing field, you'll see that it is so much more than you ever realized before.

What Satan likes to do with singles is the same thing he did with Adam and Eve. In getting them to focus on the one tree they couldn't have (the boundary line), he led them to miss out on all the trees they could have (the playing field). Satan loves to get singles to focus on the one thing they don't have (usually marriage, or it could even be sex), and they wind up missing out on maximizing, experiencing, and enjoying all they do have.

Yet one of the most beautiful things about singleness is that you are fully free.

If you could be a fly on the wall of my office the numerous times I counsel married couples, you would hear the same word I hear over and over and over again: *Trapped.* I can't tell you how many times I've been asked to help married couples not feel so trapped. One husband came to me after only six months of marriage, already saying he felt trapped and wanted out.

Kingdom single, never undervalue the gift of freedom you now have to fully live, because freedom is a gift worth more than you probably realize. Enjoy your freedom. Use your freedom wisely. Maximize your freedom and the kingdom authority that comes with it. Embrace your freedom. And discover all you can do in this season of life to become your best version of yourself. When you view freedom and completeness through the lens of God's love for you, you will truly be living as a kingdom single. Remember, a kingdom single is an unmarried Christian who is committed to fully and freely maximizing his or her completeness under the rule of God. It is God's intention for you to be single and satisfied under His authority.

You will know you're truly a kingdom single when you reach that point where, even if you want to be married someday, you don't *need* to be. There's nothing wrong with wanting to marry at some point (which was

God's ultimate plan for single people before sin entered the world). But if you're a kingdom single, you don't have to be married to feel complete and whole.

God wants every unmarried Christian to have and be fulfilled in what He gave Adam and Eve as singles, namely, His image and the divine identity within it so they would mirror God's spiritual reality. He also gave them His presence so they would live all of life in fellowship with Him. He gave them His purpose so they would do the work He had given them to do. In addition, He gave them His instructions so they would operate under divine direction and not merely by human reasoning and rationale.

As a kingdom single, you also have a divine self-image and a divinely ordained purpose to live out in fellowship with God under the authority of His divine revelation. Only when this is taking place at its fullest are you fully ready (emotionally and spiritually) to be married. Only kingdom singles can ever hope to enjoy a kingdom marriage.

Returning to our egg illustration, I'll acknowledge, like most people, that two good eggs joined together can make for a tasty omelet. Marriage can be wonderful, yes. But a single egg served over easy, sunny side up, or scrambled can be just as wonderful. Singleness affords you the unique opportunity to determine and discover what kind of eggs you truly enjoy most.

2

THE CALLING OF SINGLES

She was only 24 years old when a crown was placed on her head, signifying the start of her reign as queen. Her father, Henry VIII, had served as king in a tumultuous rule that saw the beheading of not only Elizabeth's mother, but of another of his wives as well.

When Elizabeth attained her rightful place as queen, following the death of her half-sister, Queen Mary I, she made a purposeful decision to remain single. Despite multiple efforts by advisors from within and royal leaders from without to connect her in a marriage of political convenience, Elizabeth stood her ground. In fact, one time when Parliament was pushing yet again to persuade her to marry and bear an heir to the throne, Elizabeth replied in a stately manner, "I have already joined myself in marriage to a husband, namely, the kingdom of England."

Well aware of her personal convictions, power, and influence, and how those might be jeopardized by marriage, Elizabeth embraced not only her singleness, but also her celibacy. She is recorded as having said to Parliament, "It would please me best if, at the last, a marble stone shall record that this queen, having lived such and such a time, lived and died a virgin."

Elizabeth's queenly reign lasted forty-four years in a time when the reign of kings or queens could sometimes last less than a year, and certainly usually no more than ten. Hers was an age in which England prospered not only financially, but also spiritually, socially, and creatively. The time of her rule is best known as the Elizabethan Era, or the Golden Age. Her singular dedication to the betterment of her kingdom produced some of the greatest advancements for her people that they had seen in hundreds of years.

Not only was Queen Elizabeth I the wife of her kingdom, but she was also the mother of its people, having said to Parliament, "Though after my death you may have many step dames, yet shall you never have a more natural mother unto you all." Queen Elizabeth I used her freedom from marriage to fully maximize not only her life on earth, but also the lives of countless others. She truly was a kingdom single who *committed herself to fully and freely maximizing her completeness under the rule of God*.

Single reader, you have also been gifted a season that offers a unique freedom to function in a way that contributes to God's kingdom as well. Is there a direct correlation between what you do every day and the calling you have to fulfill God's purpose in your life? Or are you allowing the world to distract you from your kingdom calling and function? Before we dive deeper into your personal calling, let's first look at the nature of the kingdom and the rule of God so we have the context within which to place your personal calling.

The Kingdom

The Greek word used for *kingdom* in the New Testament is *basileia*, which ultimately means "authority" and "rule." A kingdom always includes three fundamental components: a ruler, a realm of subjects who fall under its rule, and the rules or governances. The kingdom of God is the authoritative execution of His comprehensive rule in all creation. The kingdom agenda is simply *the visible manifestation of the comprehensive rule of God over every area of life.*[1]

God's kingdom transcends time, space, politics, denominations, cultures, and the realms of society. It is both now (Mark 1:15) and not yet (Matthew 16:28), close by (Luke 17:21) and removed (Matthew 7:21). Governed by covenantal systems, the kingdom has within it separate responsibilities and dominion, all of which are to work in conjunction with the others under divine rule and based on an absolute standard of truth. When they do, they achieve the common goal of bringing order to a world of confusion and promoting personal responsibility under God.

The primary component upon which all else rests in a kingdom is the authority of the ruler. Without that, there is anarchy resulting in mess. This is exactly why Satan's very first move in the garden was to subtly and deceitfully dethrone the ruler.

God's kingdom transcends time, space, politics, denominations, cultures, and the realms of society.

Before we ever read about Satan approaching Eve in the Garden, each reference to God in the Scriptures in relation to Adam, as a single man, is made as "LORD God." Anytime you read the word LORD (in all caps), the Hebrew term in the original text is *Yahweh*. *Yahweh* literally means "master and absolute ruler." It's the name God used to reveal Himself to mankind regarding His relationship with us. Prior to that point in Scripture, God revealed Himself as Creator, which is the Hebrew term *Elohim*.

However, when Satan spoke to Eve about eating that which she could not have, he didn't refer to God as LORD *God*. Essentially, he stripped off the name "LORD"—removing the relational aspect of "master and absolute ruler"—and instead said, "Indeed, has *God* said?"

Thus Satan sought to reduce God's rulership over and relationship with mankind by beginning with the subtle, but significant, twist in His name. In doing so, Satan kept the concept of religion while eliminating divine authority, rule, and relationship.

By removing LORD from the authoritative nature of the relationship between God and Adam and Eve, and in bypassing Adam by going directly to Eve, Satan not only caused mankind to rebel, but he also took over the dominion that man was supposed to be exercising under God's authority. When both Adam and Eve ate from the fruit in disobedience, they chose to change how they viewed their Creator from *LORD God* to just *God*, resulting in the loss of not only their intimate fellowship with Him and each other, but also of the power of the dominion that flows from the ultimate Ruler of the domain. They transitioned from a *relationship* with God to what is commonly known today as *religion*.

> *There are two answers to every question—God's answer and everyone else's. When they contradict, everyone else is wrong.*

There are two answers to every question—God's answer and everyone else's. When they contradict, everyone else is wrong. Removing the title of "master and absolute ruler" from a single's relationship to God essentially places God's answer on the same level as everyone else's. Adam's sin was in allowing a human viewpoint that had been initiated by Satan to override the revealed will and word of God. His commitment to a human love relationship was allowed to influence his spiritual decision. But unlike Adam, your desire for love as a kingdom single must never be allowed to overrule your submission to God's kingdom rule.

Singles, it is only in putting the LORD back into your relationship and identity that you will experience the freedom, purpose, completeness, dominion, and victory you were created to have. In seeking first His kingdom and His righteousness (Matthew 6:33), all other things will be given to you. You won't have to force them, find them, or fix them. They will be given.

Your Right to Rule

So much of what I've seen as casualties in the Body of Christ over the course of several decades of ministry has come as a direct result of believers not grasping and living out their God-given authority in their kingdom right to rule. Much of this breakdown is due to the church's failure to repair the damage it has done in undervaluing singles, as well as failing to reposition its singles to a place of equity and usefulness for the kingdom, both in the church and for the benefit of the broader society.

Now, you may not consider yourself a ruler. Certainly a crown doesn't sit atop your head as it did Queen Elizabeth's. But as we go through these Scripture passages, you may be surprised to discover you have been uniquely empowered to rule over a sphere of influence God has assigned to you.

Exploring the foundational theology of your spiritual authority as revealed in your right to rule will, in turn, lead you to see how the responsibility of ruling your world enables you to live fully fulfilled as a kingdom single. Understanding why you get to freely exercise your legitimate, bibliocentric rule lays the cornerstone for all else.

When God created the earth, He demonstrated His genius simply through His Word. Whatever He spoke came into being. Not only did it come into being, but it was also good. In five days, God had created a spectacular earth with all the nuances and idiosyncrasies necessary for life to be lived out to its fullest. On the sixth day, God spoke forth His crowning achievement—humanity. About humanity, we read that first,

> "God said" (Genesis 1:26),
> then, "God created" (Genesis 1:27),
> and next, "God blessed" (Genesis 1:28).

God said it, God created it, and God blessed it. Obviously, this is how God intended it. Because we are about to tread into some delicate territory,

I don't want you to just take my word for it—take His. Also in Genesis 1 we read, "Then God said, 'Let Us make man in Our image, according to Our likeness; and let them rule'" (Genesis 1:26).

On the sixth day, God created man in His own image. Both "male and female" were made in the image of God and given rulership. The plurality of "Let Us" and "Our image" refers to God's Trinitarian nature, indicating the fullness of function found in the creation of humanity as a reflection of Him. Mankind was uniquely created to mirror God's rule in the visible, physical world as it exists in the invisible, spiritual realm.

When God created humanity in His image, He delegated the responsibility to us of caring for and managing His creation. Up to that time, God did all the work. He separated the water from the land, formed the light, grew the plants, placed the stars in the sky, along with everything else. Up to then, God took care of it all through His spoken word. Yet on the sixth day, when God created man, He put the running, ruling, and stewardship of the earth into the hands of humanity. God endowed us with both the opportunity and the responsibility to manage what He had made. God gave a mandate—the dominion mandate, "Let them rule." This set in place our management over what God had created.

That is no small thing, kingdom single. Fundamentally, it is God's willing release of much of the direct control over that which He has placed on Earth while simultaneously handing that direct control to us to manage the affairs of history.

Keep in mind, this does not mean God has turned over absolute ownership of the earth. But what He has released is the managerial responsibility for ruling it. In doing this, God has established a process, within certain sovereign boundaries, whereby He respects humanity's decisions—even if those decisions go against Him, and even if those decisions are not in the best interests of what is being managed. God said, "Let them rule." While God retains absolute, sovereign authority and ownership, He has delegated relative authority to us within the sphere of influence, or dominion, that each person inhabits.

For example, the bank may own the house you live in, but it's your responsibility to pay a monthly mortgage on the house you say you "own," as well as to maintain it, for good or for bad. Now, it feels great to walk into a house you have just purchased and think, *I own this house.* But the truth is, in most cases, the bank owns that house.

The bank is not involved with the everyday duties of running your house—that's your responsibility—but the bank owns the house. Nor does the bank force you to have a clean house or prevent you from having a junky one. That's up to you. Yet, similarly, the bank does not give up ultimate ownership of the house just because you're the one living in it and managing it. If you don't make your payments, you will face the consequence of no longer occupying that house.

The same holds true in the realm where you have been assigned to rule. God is the ultimate owner. He has delegated the responsibility to manage it without having delegated His sovereignty over and within it. Your decisions directly affect the quality of life within the sphere in which you function, and they will have a large bearing on whether your realm of influence increases or decreases with time. God didn't stop Adam and Eve from eating the fruit, but He controlled the consequences when they did, thus reducing their dominion from what it had originally been ordained to be.

What Satan has done in trying to increase his influence on Earth is to cast a shadow on humanity's legitimate, God-ordained right to rule with the stained hues of complacency and insignificance. He has done this in an attempt to handcuff believers from carrying out the kingdom responsibilities given to them.

Yet David, a man after God's own heart and a king who exercised a great deal of authority, clearly articulated the high level at which God has placed humanity, for good or for bad, showing us the truth of how we are to operate within our sphere of influence. He wrote in Psalm 8:

> When I consider Your heavens, the work of Your fingers, the moon and the stars, which You have ordained; What is man that You take thought of him, And the son of man that You care for him? Yet You have made him a little lower than God, And You crown him with glory and majesty! *You make him to rule* over the works of Your hands; You have put all things under his feet. (Psalm 8:3-6, italics mine)

In this passage, David praised God not only for the greatness of His creation, but also for the glory and majesty He has given to humanity, as well as the rule He has turned over. God has placed a crown on the head of every woman and man. You are majestic. You are royalty. You are significant. You are created to be a kingdom single who is fulfilling a kingdom assignment.

The enemy, however, doesn't want you to know you are all these things. Satan doesn't want you to know you have glory, honor, and dominion that God Himself has given you to live out on Earth. As long as Satan can keep you from *thinking* like royalty, he can keep you from *acting* like royalty.

As long as he can keep you thinking that you're nobody, or that you don't matter and have no say, he can keep you acting as if you're nobody, you don't matter, and you have no say.

As a result, Satan can keep the kingdom of God from advancing as it ought to advance, because those who have been given the legitimate authority to advance it have been lulled into believing that they lack not only significance, but also dominion and authority.

Every individual piece in a checker set has a crown on it. This is because every checker has the possibility of becoming a king. Whether that happens depends on the moves that are made. Likewise, you have been crowned with majesty in God's kingdom. It's up to you to use the rights that come with the majesty you have been given. While God is the sovereign and absolute King, He has given you an area to rule in His name, by His rules, and in His image as a kingdom single.

You are a reflection of God, an image-bearer. And God has placed you, like Adam, in a "garden." You get to call the shots, for good or for bad, and how you call them will have a bearing on how chaotic or productive your garden becomes. He has given you the dominion mandate. He has said, "Let them rule . . . ." This means you have a kingdom assignment to oversee and fulfill.

> *As long as Satan can keep you from* thinking *like royalty, he can keep you from* acting *like royalty.*

God has a unique plan for you. A specific plan. Just as an appliance is uniquely equipped to fulfill its manufactured purpose, so also God has uniquely equipped you for yours.

People often ask me how to discern their personal calling. One of the ways is to identify what you've learned from past experiences, what your skills are, what your passions are (what would you do for free, even if you were not going to be paid?), what keeps you up at night thinking about it, your personality strengths, and your spiritual gifts. Then consider, where do these all converge? When you place them together in a grid, you create a matrix of meaning pointing you to your calling, the plan for which God has destined you.

Not only does God have a calling for you, but He has also given you the authority you need to perform it well. Maybe you've lost the advantage of that authority somewhere along the way through poor decisions or neglect, or maybe you've even forgotten where that authority is located. But God has a "lost and found" for you to visit in order to get back what the enemy has either tricked you out of or taken away.

As a single, it's critical to identify and live out your purpose. This is such a free season for you to explore your gifts, passions, and experiences and how they merge into your calling. Don't let other people or your own feelings of disappointment distract you from passionately pursuing your calling. Remember, the quickest way for God to get you where He wants you is for Him to be able to use you where He has you.

If you're unsure how to identify your calling, I go deeper into the subject in other books, such as *Discover Your Destiny* and *Detours*. However, as a brief overview here, let's look a bit closer at your gifts, passions, experiences, intersections, vision, and personality.

Gifts: These are the qualities that make up not only your skill set, but also your expertise and spiritual proficiencies. They can include natural talents, such as a mind for mathematics or baking, but they can also include spiritual gifts, such as mercy, faith, or leadership. God has uniquely equipped you with a set of gifts that flow more freely through you than perhaps in someone else. This combination of strengths was given for a purpose and will align with your calling.

Passions: Your passion is your "why." It's what motivates you to do what you do. When you're self-motivated, no one else needs to prod, nudge, or push you to get a job done. Your passion is often referred to as your "hunger." It's what keeps you up at night thinking or won't let you rest because you need to make a difference in this area of life. A great way to identify your passion is to ask yourself what you would do if no one were to pay you anything at all. You do it because you believe in its value, enjoy it, and desire to make the world a better place through it.

Experiences: Your experiences may seem random or disconnected at times, but our sovereign God has intentionally allowed you to go through experiences that have developed you into the person you are now. Some were positive and some were negative, but they all have crafted your mind, heart, and spirit into who you are today. Identifying patterns in past experiences, or patterns in what was learned from those experiences, and then aligning those with your gifts and passions can help you identify or confirm your calling.

Intersections: Another word we often use for intersections is *connection*, or even *networking*. It's like a highway when roads merge and you have the opportunity to cross paths with another route. These divine connections are how God brings you to your calling. Maybe it's a person you end up working for that you met in a random fashion, or a church you start attending that winds up providing a vocation. It could be a friend of a friend who introduces you to an organization for which you wind up volunteering. Whatever it is, it's not random. God has created intersections in your life to take you from point A to point Z, mile by mile. Keep your eyes open to the intersections, because they're often an indicator of direction.

Vision: Your vision is a dream that has been birthed in your heart. It's your view of the future, or something you want to accomplish. Visions come in various ways, and people can have multiple visions in their lives. Each vision serves as a guide toward living out your purpose and calling. There are steps to take in order to validate your vision, so I'm not encouraging you to simply chase any thought that comes to your head. But once you've confirmed that your vision is from God, it will be an integral part of fulfilling your destiny.

Personality: No two of us have the same personality. Some people are introverts. Others are extroverts. Some people prefer things to be in a certain order, while others prefer life to flow more randomly. Some are highly logical, while other people can be highly emotional. Whatever the case, God has uniquely designed and chosen your personality to fit the calling and destiny He's created you to fulfill. When you are living in your God-ordained purpose, you can truly be yourself in it. You don't have to try to be somebody else, because you fit perfectly into the needs and structure of what you do. You're free to be who you were created to be.

When all six of those elements come together, you will begin to experience what it is to be undivided and focused in your purpose. For example, appliances are created with a purpose. Refrigerators don't cook food. Stoves don't keep things cold. Toasters don't open cans, and can openers don't toast bread. They're all appliances, but they're not all created to accomplish the same task.

You have been uniquely created by God for the special purpose He has for you to use for His glory, your good, and the help of others. A kingdom calling will fulfill you and benefit those around you while highlighting God and His power, grace, and mercy.

Get Going

You may know your calling now, or you may simply know bits and pieces of it. Whatever it is you do know, I want to encourage you to get busy doing that. God always hits a moving target. What was Adam doing when he found a wife? He wasn't out girl watching, because there were no other human beings around. He wasn't daydreaming about his wedding day. Adam was busy functioning in his God-given role of tending the Garden of Eden and, more specifically, naming the animals.

Likewise, God doesn't want you sitting around, so focused on your wedding day that you miss out on the pleasures and purpose He has for you today. He wants you functioning for Him until, or even if, He creates your wedding day. He wants you fully thriving in your purpose right now.

My parents used to take my siblings and me for Sunday afternoon drives. The goal was just to go, not to go anywhere in particular. That was fun for a while, but then it became boring.

Are you going through life aimlessly, or do you have a mission and sense of calling on your life? Do you have a passion from God that motivates you? If you're a single Christian, it's because God has you single, and you ought to know why He wants you to function in this calling for whatever period He deems right since you are already complete in Him.

Living freely and fully for Christ in your calling as an unmarried believer will require a change of your focus—from preoccupation with marriage, your past, future, lack, or desires to a preoccupation with Jesus and His purpose for your life. Paul wrote in 1 Corinthians 7:35, "This I say for your own benefit; not to put a restraint upon you, but to promote what is appropriate and to secure undistracted devotion to the Lord."

When Lois and I travel to New York every spring, we usually like to spend some time shopping on and around Fifth Avenue. One day when we were there, we passed a large group of people who were staring at a display window in the Macy's store. Curious as to why the group had gathered, we walked over to check it out.

There in the display window stood some mannequins showing off the newest styles and trends of the season. Looking as closely as I could, I still couldn't figure out what had drawn the enormous crowd. It looked like a typical display window. That is, until I started to notice some of the people in the crowd making faces and large gestures to the mannequins. That struck me as odd, but then it dawned on me that one of the mannequins wasn't really a mannequin after all. It was a woman dressed up and standing perfectly still with the mannequins.

The onlookers were trying desperately to distract her and get her to move, to no avail. This is because the woman knew that her obligation was to another kingdom—a kingdom called Macy's—and not to the crowd seeking to draw her attention away from her focus. Similarly, the Lord desires your undistracted devotion to Him as a member of His kingdom. Although the world and its fanfare may seek to draw you away, your commitment to Him ought always to remain as your number one priority.

Paul was not trying to handcuff single Christians and keep the two sexes apart in what he wrote. He wasn't trying to prevent people from desiring to get married or pursuing matrimony. He wasn't anti-marriage at all. But there's a benefit in being single that Paul wanted to make sure his readers understood as well. This benefit is "undistracted devotion to the Lord." One way Satan robs us of God's best is to cause a disturbance in our lives to distract us, much the way one thief may distract a store clerk so the other thief can steal merchandise or money without being noticed.

In bowling, every lane is occupied by a single bowler. That bowler's total focus needs to be on the impact he or she can make. The moment that bowler starts noticing what's happening with other bowlers on other lanes, he will mess up his own ability to have his own impact, or she may even wind up rolling gutter balls.

I understand that in our world of social media consumption, comparisons happen daily, if not hourly. But the measurement of your life as a single is not to be compared with other singles, or even married couples.

God has a purpose for you, and it won't line up with His purpose for others.

God has a purpose for you, and it won't line up with His purpose for others. Seize the days you have as a single, and avoid the temptation of distraction through comparison during this season of your life.

Satan uses comparison to disturb so many Christian singles and worry them about their marital status or being "incomplete" that he's running amok through their lives, stealing their joy and robbing them of their effectiveness for Christ. When your focus shifts from Christ to yourself, a thief is at work on you, seeking to rob you of your sense of completeness as a kingdom single.

Paul's point in 1 Corinthians 7 is that married people, by virtue of being married, are divided. They have divided responsibilities. They need to please their spouse, fulfill their purpose, and please God. They're constantly shifting among different focuses, because the very nature of the relationships forces the division.

But a Christian single is undivided.

So many singles today are frustrated, however, because they're experiencing as a single what they should be experiencing only if they were married: They're divided. By being consumed with thoughts about marriage, dating, finding a mate, and sex, they're living under the strain of divided responsibilities. If God hasn't given you a mate to worry about yet, leave that person alone in your priorities, time, and thoughts. Because that person doesn't exist yet. Keep the desire, lose the distraction.

I advise singles who are struggling with the overwhelming desire for marriage to take one meal or day a week to fast and pray about their desire. Then don't revisit the issue until the following week. This way they are spiritually addressing the issue without being consumed by it.

The moment you're divided emotionally and spiritually, you have let your singleness get in the way of God's kingdom calling for your life and well-being. If you're spending an inordinate amount of time thinking about marriage, looking at wedding dresses, watching television programs about people getting married or being married, dating person after person, or scrolling through screens of prospects online, and as a result you're feeling frustrated and distracted, you have been pulled away from a spiritual focus.

A successful kingdom single is one who seeks to maximize his or her singleness for the betterment of self and others, the advancement of God's kingdom, and the manifestation of His glory.

Here's the question every single should ask: "God, how do You want me to use the state I'm in until You change my state for Your maximum purpose?" When God answers that question—even though the desire to be married may still remain—you will have a passion and a purpose that will supersede any dominating thoughts you once held for marriage.

It's easy to become distracted by unhealthy relationships, television programs, and even personal discouragement. However, God is trying to get your attention so you can experience all the fullness He has in store for you in this phase of your life. During this time of singleness, you should be preparing yourself emotionally and spiritually in order to become the best you that you can be. You don't just want to avoid marrying the wrong person someday; you want to avoid being the wrong person if and when you do get married. That requires time to focus on the race God has mapped out for your own spiritual growth.

This reminds me of an incident that happened many years ago in an international track and field meet. During the four-by-one-hundred relay, a Jamaican athlete who was to run the third leg of the race for his team allowed his attention to wander as he waited for the baton to be passed.

This man happened to look up at the big screen that was televising another event, and he saw a friend getting ready to compete. The runner stared at the screen for just a few seconds, but as he did, his teammate came running up to him with the baton. Instead of making a smooth handoff, the incoming runner collided with his distracted teammate, and the race was over for the Jamaican team.

The message for us is clear. We need to stop looking at other people's races and start running our own. For singles, this includes keeping your focus on God instead of always looking around for a partner. Or looking around at your friends who may be getting married before you, or who may have found a contented romantic relationship. That's their race, not yours. God is saying to you, "Focus on Me, and I'll do your looking for you."

I love the story of the businessman and the Native American who were walking down a noisy city street one day. Suddenly, the Native American stopped and said, "Shhh. Listen!"

The businessman asked, "Listen for what?"

"Don't you hear it?" the Native American replied. "It's a cricket."

The businessman said, "A cricket? I don't hear anything."

But the Native American looked around and saw a cricket on the sidewalk. He reached down, picked it up, and showed it to the businessman, who was amazed.

"I don't believe it," the businessman said. "Here we are downtown, with all this noise and all these people, and you hear a cricket. How did you do that?"

"I'll show you," the other man said. He took some change out of his pocket and threw it on the sidewalk. As the money clattered and rolled around, twenty people stopped to look. "You always hear what you're tuned in to hear," the Native American said.

Many singles will never find their mates because they're tuned into their friends, the dating scene, or something else instead of being tuned into God. But He's the only One who knew how to get Adam and Eve together, or even knew where both were located.

Kingdom single, if you'll set your focus on God and function for Him in the freedom He's given you, you won't have to worry about His finding you when He's ready to link you with someone. Look to God, and let Him do your looking for you.

One day way back before cellphones and texting, I was at the airport trying to get to the gate for my next flight when I heard over the intercom, "Dr. Tony Evans, please go to the nearest white courtesy phone for a message."

I was concentrating on something else, because I had a flight to make and a destination to reach, so it took a few seconds for the reality to sink in that I was the one being paged. I went to the nearest phone and received a message from my assistant, who needed to tell me about a sudden change in my travel arrangements. She knew I was still at the airport, because she organizes my schedule.

My point is that this phone call found me in the middle of thousands of people who also had flights to make and plans to keep. I was

If God wants to interrupt your plans and call your name with a message, He knows how to reach you.

doing what I was called to do, on my way to minister the Word of God to people. I didn't go to the airport to hang out and wait for a call from my assistant. But when she needed to reach me, it was no problem because she knew where I was and because the airport has a system in place to reach travelers with important messages. The fact that I was immersed in a sea of people in the middle of a noisy terminal was no obstacle at all.

God has sent you to the airport because He wants to take you somewhere and has a plan to get you there. And when you as a kingdom single decide you're going to focus on Christ and His plan and purpose for you, if God wants to interrupt your plans and call your name with a message, He knows how to reach you. He knows how to divert you. He can track you down, call you by name, and set you off in an entirely different direction from what you even knew was possible.

In the meantime, if He hasn't yet called to connect you with your future mate, your role is to keep your focus on Him and keep moving ahead with His calling for you right now. When you're going somewhere with the Lord, getting ready to fly high with Him in your calling under His rule, He is freed up to make a connection both with you and for you.

One of my favorite movies is *The Matrix*. It's about a man who lives and works as a computer programmer by day and a hacker by night. Then one day, during his normal, routine life, he's introduced to a group of people who give him an option to leave the realm of the "known" and enter a realm where power, influence, notoriety, and the ability to become a hero are afforded to him.

In one scene, Thomas Anderson (the main character) is sitting across from the man who is inviting him to leave the known world and enter the world of the matrix. The man offers Anderson either a red pill or a blue pill. If Anderson chooses the blue pill, he is guaranteed a safe return to his safe, comfort-zone world that he has always known. If he chooses the red pill, he will be whisked away from that world and enter a new kingdom, and thus be given the opportunity to save the world he's leaving from certain doom. If you've seen the movie or any of its sequels, you know he chose the red pill.

What you may not have remembered, however, is that it was only after Anderson chose his higher calling that he met the love of his life. Her name was Trinity, and she was waiting for him outside the confines of his comfortable, predictable life. In chasing after the purpose established for him, Thomas Anderson gained more than meaning and destiny, he gained a love he'd only dreamed was possible. Similarly, God gave Adam a kingdom calling and assignment before He ever gave him a wife.

Friend, your completeness as a kingdom single is first and foremost found in your passionate, all-consuming pursuit of God's kingdom purpose and calling, not in your formal connection with another person. But chase your calling endowed upon you by your Creator and you just may be surprised to discover that it comes with a companion who will help you live it out even better than you ever could have on your own.

3
〜◇〜

THE CONFIDENCE
OF SINGLES

An air of electricity and excitement wafted over my wife and me as we walked into the Richard Rodgers Theatre on Broadway not too long ago. If you have also walked into this theater within the last few years, you know exactly what I mean.

Just getting a ticket to enter often requires moving both heaven and earth, mortgaging your home, or dipping into the kids' college fund. Yet based on the faces flush with delight as ballads, choreography, and an infectious storyline of intrigue swept us all up in a momentum of unending movement, it was worth it.

My wife and I have seen many Broadway musicals in our day (far too many to count), but *Hamilton* left a lasting impression and had a powerful impact on my mind and my emotions.

What I would have given to be a fly on the wall during the rehearsals for this historic production! To experience the trial and error of lines, locations, songs, and more would have been interesting, to say the least. I wonder what the producers, actors, and investors thought as they spent weeks or months, even, of ten-hour days and more than $12 million preparing for the opening night. Did they know it would be the success it has become? Did they expect such unprecedented greatness? Did they see something beyond their off-Broadway debut in the Public Theater? Did they expect more dollar digits on the ticket stubs one day?

I imagine they did. I also imagine that's why they were willing to pour so much time, money, and effort into massaging this musical into the masterpiece it has become.

After all, expectations affect behavior. If you expect to not only recoup your $12 million investment, but also to generate a billion dollars in profit at some point, you'll put in all that's necessary to achieve that goal. If you expect to be a doctor, you'll go to medical school. If you expect to be a lawyer, you'll attend law school. If you expect to be a professional athlete, you'll exercise your body day in and day out, morning, noon, and night, because you know that kind of training is required for you to reach your expectations. What's more, if you expect to one day be inducted into the hall of fame, you'll give all you've got on every single play, regardless of the score and regardless of any pain you may have to push through.

Expectations determine behavior.

This is why it's critical as a kingdom single to live in light of great expectations—not only for your life on Earth, but also and more importantly, for eternity. The greater your expectations are of heaven, the better life you will experience on Earth. The lower your expectations are of heaven, the lesser the life you'll experience on Earth.

The greater your expectations are of heaven, the better life you will experience on Earth.

Thus, if you really want to maximize the time given to you on Earth, you must learn to live with eternity in mind. The problems so many people face today arise out of an expectation that this life is all there is. They toss their entire bag of marbles into history, all the while missing what heaven has in store and how heaven ought to dictate our expectations and actions in history.

This is particularly true in relation to how we manage and view our time. Time is important. It can often seem there's never enough of it. And at other times, it seems to drag on for way too long. But how you view time, as a kingdom single, may be far more important than you realize.

In the book of 2 Peter, we gain valuable insight into the true dynamic and nature of our time when we read, "But do not let this one fact escape your notice, beloved, that with the Lord one day is like a thousand years, and a thousand years like one day" (3:8). Try not to gloss over that too quickly and fail to engage its depth. We live our lives linearly, from one point in time to the next. From one birthday to the next birthday. Or from one paycheck to the next paycheck. Or one relationship to the next relationship. We move from seconds to minutes to hours to months, and even years and decades. That's how we measure time. That's how we measure our lives.

Yet God does not operate by linear time at all. In other words, He transcends time, which is why Scripture calls Him the *eternal* God. Rather than being bound as we are in three phases—what was, what is, and what is to come (yesterday, today, and tomorrow)—God sits outside of everything but Himself. He doesn't have a yesterday, nor does He face a tomorrow. Every single moment to God is simply: NOW. It is His. And it is Him.

When Moses met God at the site of the burning bush and received his call to proclaim release for God's people in Egypt, he asked God to tell him who He was. We read, "Then Moses said to God, 'Behold, I am going to the sons of Israel, and I will say to them, "The God of your fathers has sent me to you." Now they may say to me, "What is His name?" What shall I say to them?'" (Exodus 3:13). The Lord responded to Moses that he should tell them, "'I AM WHO I AM' . . . 'Thus you shall say to the sons of Israel, "I AM has sent me to you"'" (verse 14).

Breaking this down in a way we can understand literally means:

I AM (present tense), defined by:

I (personal pronoun) and AM (present tense).

In other words, God only IS. He exists now, has always existed now, and will always exist now. That's why time will be meaningless to you and me in eternity—because time is meaningless to the ever-present God. There will be no night. There will be only day. There will be no sunset. There will be no sunrise. There will be no seasons nor any other measurements of time. The popular Christian song "I Can Only Imagine" inspires us to imagine how eternity might be, but a concept of timelessness is simply beyond the grasp of most, if not all, of our imaginations. You might go crazy if you spend too much time trying to figure out *time*.

So in an effort to explain this unexplainable reality in a way we can grasp, God gave us the illustration we looked at earlier: *With the Lord, one day is like a thousand years, and a thousand years are like one day.* Translation: Don't use your watch to measure God's time. You just can't do it. It's outside you. It's beyond your imagination. It's why He is the great, "unfigureoutable" God that He is. Or, as Isaiah put it, " 'For My thoughts are not your thoughts, nor are your ways My ways,' declares the LORD. 'For as the heavens are higher than the earth, so are My ways higher than your ways and My thoughts than your thoughts'" (Isaiah 55:8-9).

Don't use your watch to measure God's time.

This reminds me of the humorous story of the man who died, went to heaven, and ran into the apostle Peter. After witnessing all the extraordinary things Peter did in heaven, the man decided to ask a question. "Hey, Pete," the man said, "how much is a minute worth up here?"

Peter looked at the man and replied without hesitation, "A minute is worth a million years."

"Wow," the man replied, clearly impressed. "And how much is a nickel worth up here?"

Peter responded just as quickly, "A nickel is worth a million dollars!"

The man started to put two and two together, and he decided to try to maximize his situation. "Pete," he asked, sporting a huge grin, "how about lending me a nickel?"

Peter smiled and replied, "Sure, no problem. Just give me a minute."

Comparing nickels to millions and minutes to millennia is like comparing apples to oranges. It simply won't equate, because it's a completely different orientation. It's like how things appear if you're driving to work on a downtown highway with a large number of other cars, bumper to bumper the whole way. You become consumed with the starting and stopping, or moving in and out of traffic. It can appear to be nothing short of chaos.

But if you were to look at the same road from an airplane window, it would all look perfectly in order, with straight lines and peaceful-appearing drivers navigating organized-looking vehicles. It's a completely different picture. This is similar to what God is asking us to do while living on Earth. He wants us to live from the vantage point of eternity, and not from the view of our bumper-to-bumper temporal existence. We're to think of heaven while we maneuver in history.

Scripture steps further into this concept with the next verse from the passage we're studying in 2 Peter: "The Lord is not slow about His promise, as some count slowness, but is patient toward you, not wishing for any to perish but for all to come to repentance" (3:9). In this passage on time, we're reminded that God is not slow about what He promises. But we confuse His perfect timing with our own perception of time.

When you judge God's timetable because it differs from your own desires for when He will act, you're using your own calculator and calendar, not His. You're seeking to hold the God of the universe, who is unbound by time, to the confines of time as you know it. That's kind of like demanding that a song be expressed in one note, and you get to pick that note. It would no longer be a song but rather an isolated sound.

God sits outside of time, and because He does, He's able to interlace all things throughout time into a cohesive whole within time. As a result, His infinite wisdom creates more than just songs or notes. He creates lives, families, communities, churches, countries, movements, continents, and an entire world into a meaningful, interconnected symphony. When we seek to hold God to our understanding and expectation of time with regard to the things in our lives, we have forgotten that our lives include more than just *our* lives.

Romans 8:28 reminds us that God works *all* things together for His good to those who love Him. Living in light of this eternal viewpoint is the only way to make sense of what often seems senseless and random in life. This is because an eternal viewpoint requires faith in a God who not only knows what the highest good is for all involved, but also knows how to bring it about for all involved. Without faith, it is impossible to please God and to enter into the full expression of His rewards (Hebrews 11:6). This is because faith requires that you take Him at His word.

Any time you or I depend on our five senses to analyze or believe something related to God, we're not fully engaging our faith. Faith means we act as if we believe God is telling the truth, regardless of what we see, hear, feel, or touch. Because He *is* telling the truth. And His Word is clear: The Lord is not slow about His promise. He will carry out His plan. He will bring about His deliverance. He will usher you into your destiny. He will supply that mate, those children, the job, finances, health—whatever the "it" is that you're seeking from Him. If and when that "it" aligns with His will for your life, *it* will happen. It just may not happen on the date or moment that you wish it to happen. You may—like the choreographers, actors, and

> *Faith means we act as if we believe God is telling the truth, regardless of what we see, hear, feel, or touch.*

musicians who were perpetually rehearsing *Hamilton* to an empty theater until opening night—simply have to keep going.

But here's the kicker: You have to (as they did) keep going strong.

If the cast and crew of *Hamilton* had decided, in their frustration over rehearsing with no audience to watch them, that they didn't want to invest well in the time given to them before opening night, they would not have been prepared to perform when it came time to do so. The play would have bombed, and most likely it would never have even made it to off of off-Broadway.

Far too many singles fail to comprehend this, so they don't keep investing strongly in their lives. Rather, they find themselves in a state of perpetual do-nothingness while waiting for their anticipated opening night. Until they get the romantic partner, or the marriage, or the family they desire, they simply just hold tight. They don't make choices, invest their time, or strengthen and polish themselves in light of their hopes, expectations, and God's promises. They sit around and complain, or they give in to a cycle of distractions to ease their minds from that which they crave. Or—worse yet—they wind up settling for an off-off-off-off-Broadway start to their future, which ultimately never takes them to Broadway at all.

Living with an eternal perspective never means sitting still and doing nothing. As a single, if you have hopes of a different sort of future than what you're experiencing right now, invest in those hopes. For example, if your desire is to give yourself physically pure to the person you will one day marry and be madly in love with, align your actions with that desire and avoid giving yourself physically to anyone else before then. That's just one example of staying strong now, but there are many. Invest in your own spiritual development, career, character, and even your own finances. Use this time to become the best version of yourself that you can by pursuing passionately what God wants you to be.

Wouldn't you want someone else to do the same for you instead of just bumbling along until you meet? Let eternal expectations drive you to discover your role in God's kingdom expansion on Earth, and pursue all that's necessary to carry it out. Be diligent to live wholly, fully, and committed as a disciple of Christ, particularly at this time as a single since this is when you're the most available to follow Him (1 Corinthians 7:34).

Personal development requires movement. It requires practice, exercise, investment, nourishment, and obedience while both understanding and carrying out God's will.

God's Rule, Our Responsibility

Over the years, I've noticed a theological conundrum that often trips people up. It exists between the two realities of God's sovereign providence and our personal responsibility. It exists between His promises and our participation. It's this theological tension between a God who is in control of everything and what that God expects from you and me. Because, after all, if He's in control of everything, and if He's not slow regarding His promises and plan for our lives, why doesn't everything seem to happen as it's supposed to?

The answer to that is in knowing that God has intentionally grafted our responsibility into His sovereignty. Some people call it free will. Others may refer to it as faith. Still others could call it obedience versus rebellion, or simply discipleship versus apathy. The best way I know how to illustrate it is through football.

In every football game, certain things are non-negotiable. The goal line, for example, is non-negotiable. You can't move it, ignore it, or do anything to it. The goal line is a sovereign line. Similarly, the goal posts are also sovereign. They don't budge.

And yet the activity on the field is up for grabs to some extent. Of course, the activity on the field must remain between the boundary lines and follow a rule book and those who interpret it (the referees). But progress on the field largely lies with the coaches and players themselves. If a team's player legally crosses the goal line with the football, the promise is six points. That promise stands. It never changes. But how, when, or even *if* the team has a player cross the goal line is up to the team. This is because within the sovereignty of the game rest the responsibilities of the players.

Let's walk this illustration back into Bible times for more clarity. As the crow flies, it was roughly a thirty-five-day journey from Egypt to the Promised Land for Moses and the millions escaping slavery and oppression. The Promised Land had been promised. So why didn't those who were people of the promise get there for another forty years? *Because they chose to view the journey through the lens of life on Earth, rather than through the lens of eternity.* They chose to view the obstacles through their own grids rather than through God's viewpoint. They chose to complain rather than to have faith and give thanks.

What they did (and did not do) affected how long it actually took to reach their promise.

You probably know the story already, but Abraham and Sarah and God's promise of a son are another perfect example of delaying the fulfillment of a promise, this time by twenty-five years (Genesis 15-18, 21). What should have happened a lot earlier was held up by their lack of faith, and by their lack of actions predicated on that faith. Keep in mind, this didn't change what God had said. It just changed how long it took to experience the manifestation of what God had said.

Some of you may have been waiting on God for decades for something He's not ready to do because you won't walk in faith. He's willing to do it for you, but He's also waiting to see whether you will trust Him enough to obey Him. To see whether you'll seek Him enough not to settle for what's immediately in front of you when what you know you're waiting for hasn't shown up yet. Or if you will go too far in that relationship physically because it's been so long since you've experienced closeness with anyone, or you think it may keep the other person around. Or whether you will passionately pursue the purpose He has for you rather than living drained in an emotional state of unending unknown, lack, and *want*.

Scripture describes countless situations demonstrating the principle that we must do something first to reveal our faith before God will do what He has said. He wants to see obedience before He answers. So all that time you may spend wondering or even saying, "God, why won't You do this, that, or the other," God is shaking His head and replying, "I will. I'm just waiting to see if you believe Me."

Consider school as another example. There's a prescribed time to finish first through twelfth grade, or to get your bachelor's or master's degree. But if you don't do the work, pass the tests, show up, and fulfill the obligations, the prescribed time that passed isn't enough to get the diploma. No school will force a degree on you simply because you "should have" gotten it in a certain amount of time.

Neither will God force His preferred will on you, or the desired answers to your prayers, just because it's been "long enough" of a wait in your mind. God sits outside time. He can wait. He's not in any hurry at all. It is only we who stay His hand when we refuse to live our lives in light of His eternal plan, honoring Him with our thoughts, words, choices, discipline, diligence, and actions.

Expect God to keep His promise to you—His promise that you have a good future filled with hope (Jeremiah 29:11). And let that confident expectation positively affect your decisions as a kingdom single each and every day. By doing so, you may even move His hand. And even if things never change in this life regarding your single status, you will be able to say like the apostle Paul, "I have fought the good fight, I have finished the course, I have kept the faith . . . there is laid up for me the crown of righteousness" (2 Timothy 4:7-8). You will enter into the presence of your Lord to receive your reward as a victorious kingdom single.

4
ᴄᴏᴏ

THE COMMAND
OF SINGLES

Some time ago, Lois and I took a much-anticipated trip to Hawaii. This came after an especially long several months with a heavy work schedule, so we were really looking forward to some peace, rest, and quiet. We couldn't wait to see the refreshing views and hear the calming sounds of the sea. I had been scheduled to preach at a conference in Hawaii, so we maximized the opportunity by tagging on a few vacation days afterward. When we boarded our flight, we were tired and worn out. But we knew that once we got there, all would be well.

We were wrong.

It didn't take more than a few minutes after unpacking our bags to discover that the resort hotel where we were staying was having some issues. Apparently, they were undergoing a major renovation and hadn't bothered to let us know. Sounds of clanging hammers and power saws screeched and banged seemingly nonstop from the time we arrived until late each evening. The noise overtook the sounds of the ocean waves, needless to say, and distracted us from what we had come there to do—rest and recoup in order to move forward strong.

To top it off, toward the end of this already chaotic trip I wound up so sick that I had to be rushed to the hospital. I had never experienced that level of pain before. I remember sitting in the car on the frantic drive to the hospital, doubled over and with tears in my eyes, thinking, *This isn't how Hawaii is supposed to be.* It was awful. They ended up admitting me to the hospital and doing surgery, and I stayed there a couple days, which wasn't much worse than the noise and clamor of the hotel.

By the time Lois and I boarded the plane back to Dallas, we were worse off than when we had left. What was supposed to have been an enjoyable vacation turned out to be miserable.

Many singles feel that way about the Christian life. They've heard all this good stuff about Jesus. They've heard about a peace that passes understanding. They've heard that the joy of the Lord is our strength, and that He has come to give life and give it more abundantly. And yet this beautiful thing called Christianity just doesn't seem to be much fun. Fully and freely enjoying your life as a kingdom single, when outside stuff is ruining your outlook and internal emotions are bringing you down, seems to leave a person empty, helpless, and in a passive state of mind.

In fact, far too many singles are living in a cycle of perpetual defeat—never able to overcome, simply subject to life's circumstances. In this manner, a feeling of helplessness to do anything about the mess and misery smothers hope. It creates a life of endurance rather than a life of exploration, where just getting through the day becomes an accomplishment in itself.

Truth be told, many singles are unhappy Christians who believe the right stuff but are finding that it just doesn't work when it comes to them. They say "amen" to the right things, affirm the right doctrines, yet locating the greatness of God that they talk and sing about looms out of reach. One reason this reality rings true for so many singles is that there's a disconnect between the spiritual authority that belongs to every believer and the actual accessing of that authority.

The concepts of singleness and authority don't tend to naturally pair up. Our culture has trained us into recognizing the power of a group. Being single can often lead to feelings of loneliness, isolation, and even inadequacy. These are not accurate definitions of singleness, but they are common, recurring associations with it. The concept of a *strong single* rarely comes up. Rather, we hear about the *struggling single* or the *waiting single* or the *stuck single*, as if being single lacks an essential component necessary for a full life. Because of this, owning and exercising spiritual authority may seem like a foreign concept altogether.

Many singles are unhappy Christians who believe the right stuff but are finding that it just doesn't work when it comes to them.

You may be surprised to discover, however, that singles have a unique opportunity to live a life of spiritual authority. This is because of the freedom found in individual stewardship. Whether that freedom involves a greater opportunity to focus, to develop yourself, or even to take risks of faith, singleness positions each person for a wonderful season of spiritual depth and authority.

When God created Adam and placed him in the Garden, He gave him authority as a single. Adam's authority extended over the realm God had placed him within, and it involved naming the creatures that had also been placed there. Adam's authority didn't come into play simply when he became connected with Eve. Rather, it was tied to him individually and remained his even after marriage. Remember our definition of a kingdom single? A kingdom single is *an unmarried Christian who is committed to fully and freely maximizing his or her completeness under the rule of God and the lordship of Jesus Christ.*

That's why, when Adam and Eve sinned against God, God did not call out, "Adam and Eve, where are y'all?" No, He said, "Adam, where are you?" (Genesis 3:9). This is because with authority comes responsibility.

Similarly, as a kingdom single, you have been endowed with authority.

Your spiritual authority allows you to have command over your realm of influence. However, accessing that command requires two critical components: faith and forgiveness.

Faith

Jesus shared great insight on this when traveling with His disciples to and from Jerusalem, as recorded in Mark 11. We read,

> On the next day, when they had left Bethany, He became hungry. Seeing at a distance a fig tree in leaf, He went to see if perhaps He would find anything on it; and when He came to it, He found nothing but leaves, for it was not the season for figs. He said to it, "May no one ever eat fruit from you again!" And His disciples were listening. (Mark 11:12-14)

The story continues a few verses later:

> As they were passing by in the morning, they saw the fig tree withered from the roots up. Being reminded, Peter said to Him, "Rabbi, look, the fig tree which You cursed has withered." And Jesus answered saying to them, "Have faith in God. Truly I say to you, whoever says to this mountain, 'Be taken up and cast into the sea,' and does not doubt in his heart, but believes that what he says is going to happen, it will be granted him. Therefore, I say to you, all things for which you pray and ask, believe that you have received them, and they will be granted you." (Mark 11:20-24)

Jesus often used natural scenarios to teach His disciples important life lessons, as He did in this case. When He first saw the fig tree, He expected to find fruit because it had leaves. But there was no fruit. Jesus then cursed the tree for giving the impression of fruitfulness without the presence of fruit, which related to the emptiness of Judaism. The next day, when the disciples passed the tree again, Peter noticed it had died. Talk about a quick turnaround! When Peter and the disciples pointed out to Jesus what had happened, He answered the question behind their statement. His answer? Faith.

For that much to happen that fast required faith.

I imagine that Jesus, knowing the full power and authority of God, must have thought that the fig tree's withering and dying was such a small example. After all, He went on to give the disciples an even larger example as He told them that with faith, someone could even tell a mountain to be cast into the sea, and it would be done. In fact, He referenced the Mount of Olives in the distance. Moving from figs to olives, Jesus assured His followers that nothing is out of reach for the power and authority of God.

Even deeper, though, the symbolism of a mountain in biblical times, culture, and language referred to something that loomed immovable (Zechariah 4:7). It related to a circumstance that was too challenging to overcome, a precipice you couldn't climb over, or an issue so firmly rooted for an extended period that it owned territory in your life and mind. For us today, a mountain has similar connotations. It symbolizes that which we can't fix, change, reverse, or do much of anything about.

As I spend time with singles in counseling or in ministry, some of these mountains I often hear spoken about are mountains of debt from living on a solitary income, mountains of past shame or regret, mountains of inhibition in future relationships through possible sexually transmitted diseases they are still carrying, or mountains of children born outside marriage. There are mountains of low self-esteem erected by a culture that promotes and promises love. Mountains of loneliness, apathy, and simply feeling overwhelmed. In addition, mountains of mistrust loom large, too.

But Jesus said clearly that all those mountains *can* move. In addition,

He went on to say we are given authority not only to speak to God about the mountains, but also to address the mountains directly.

God is just waiting on you to say the word, infused with faith, of course.

So why are more kingdom singles not seeing the mountains moved in their lives, relationships, careers, or circumstances? Because fundamentally they don't have the faith it takes to do so. Spiritual authority, the right to use divine power, is accessed through faith alone—actual faith, not just words of faith or semblances of faith, which are like the leaves on that fig tree that purported to indicate fruit. Spiritual authority is only accessed through faith.

One of the best ways I know to illustrate this is in the power source in your home or apartment. That power comes to you through your contract with the utility company. This formal, legal relationship with your electricity provider grants you access to power.

Spiritual authority is only accessed through faith.

Yet power that's *available* for your house does not equal power that is *utilized* in your house. This is because you can have access to power but not use it. For the power to be manifested and actualized in your home, you have to meet a responsibility. If you don't flip on a switch, plug in a piece of equipment, or pay your bill, that power will go unused. It won't go unused because it's not there. It will go unused because it's not accessed. Thus, you'll live in darkness not for a lack of power, but rather for a lack of accessing that power.

Many Christian singles are asking God, "Why aren't You giving me power to live in this season of my life with victory?" Meanwhile, God is asking them, "Why aren't you flipping the switch of faith? Why aren't you exercising My power through the authority that's yours? Why are you not speaking to the mountain under My authority?"

Let's take this one step further. Suppose you called your electric company and said, "I don't have any light in my home. Will you please turn on my lights?"

You would hear a pause and then an answer: "I'm sorry, but we don't turn on the lights. We supply the power to the lights so that when you turn them on, there will be light."

Far too many believers are looking for power, asking God for power, and whining about not having enough power, when they ought to be exercising access to the power that has been supplied them. It is in our refusal as believers to exercise kingdom authority that we make ourselves impotent concerning any power.

When the power has already been provided through Christ's death, burial, and resurrection, you have access to unlimited authority simply through faith. That's why knowing God is so critical. Much of the faith we think we have is faith in faith, not faith in God. It's in a god we made up who exists within our framework and understanding, and under the power of our manipulation. It's not faith in God as He reveals Himself to be, but rather in a god as we wish He were.

See, the issue with faith is never about the size of your faith. You should never wish you had "more faith." A grain the size of a mustard seed will do. The issue of faith lies in the worthiness of its object. For example, let's say I have a lot of faith in the Tooth Fairy—or even in Cupid or Santa Claus. But the amount of my faith in any of those things is irrelevant simply because the object of that faith is unworthy of my confidence in it. The object itself is inauthentic.

Moving mountains by faith doesn't take a ton of faith. In fact, a little dab will do you. What it does take is the placement of that faith in the one and only God who can move those mountains. Thus, the reason you need to know God well is that you need to know His character, His Word, and His promises. You need to know what you can honestly expect from Him, because if you don't know what you can expect from Him, you may be believing Him for something you should not be believing Him for, because

His Word and character never said He'd provide it. Only as there is legitimate faith in God do you get to exercise legitimate command on Earth. If you have illegitimate faith in God because you have misunderstood, misinterpreted, or failed to know His promises, you cannot exercise authority.

Yet when you have faith in the veracity of the God of the Bible, you can simply command whatever mountain you are facing in your life to move, and it will move. Jesus said in the passage we looked at earlier, "Therefore, I say to you, all things for which you pray and ask, believe that you have received them, and they will be granted you." Now, any grammarian or copy editor may have taken a red pen to that passage. After all, it contains three different tenses:

Present tense: All things for which you pray and ask, believe

Present perfect tense: that you have received them,

Future tense: and they will be granted you.

This present-, present perfect-, and future-tense reality of faith and prayer is something we often overlook. But it holds the key to accessing your spiritual authority.

Let me ask you a question: When you believe you "have received" something, how does that affect your emotions, actions, and thoughts? For example, if you ordered a hamburger at a drive-through window, how would believing that the reception of that hamburger was a "done deal" impact your actions? If you doubted, would you drive up to the next window, or possibly pull away? Would you pay ahead of time, or be hesitant to pay at all? Would you start salivating on the way to the second window, or still focus on the hunger pangs gnawing inside you?

Believing that something is a "done deal" affects everything. That's faith.

Putting it in the context of singleness, if you pray for a godly mate and that God will introduce you to him or her, and if you believe this answer is a "done deal" based on God's Word, do you still need to go to the club? Do you still need to worry about the clock ticking away? Do you give yourself away sexually to someone you're just dating? Or are you more apt to move forward in your life—do things like repair your credit score, remove your debt, get physically fit, mentally plan your honeymoon, take those extra classes to finish your master's degree, and more—if you know this is a "done deal"?

What happens too often in prayer is that we lack the faith to believe we have received our request. So while we tell the mountain to move, we also pick up a chisel and start carving into it ourselves. Or while we curse the fig tree, we seek to dig it up too. All this effort we direct at doing and thinking the wrong things keeps us in that perpetual state known as being "stuck." And it keeps God's answer at bay because He sees our lack of faith. Commanding spiritual authority not only involves accessing God's power through faith, but also taking responsibility to act according to that faith.

In the Israelites' early days in the Promised Land after wandering the wilderness, God told Joshua, "Every place on which the sole of your foot treads, I have given it to you" (Joshua 1:3). This was God's promise to Joshua. But Joshua's enacting and living out of his faith involved actual walking. He couldn't sit at home in his tent, prop up his feet, and say, "Well, the Lord has given me everything, why should I bother? I'm just going to relax today." No, Joshua needed to put in the effort of faith, which meant doing what God had instructed him to do. He had to walk to the places he wanted to receive. He had to put the sole of his foot on the very property itself.

> *Faith is more than a feeling. Faith involves your feet.*

Friend, faith is more than a feeling. Faith involves your feet. It involves actions, thoughts, and words that align with the belief you have regarding the situation about which you have the faith.

If those things don't align, you aren't exercising faith.

Romans 3:27 tells us, "Where then is boasting? It is excluded. By what kind of law? Of works? No, but by a law of faith." Just as there is a law of gravity by which tangible, physical items are held in place, so also faith is a law. Faith is a rule of operation.

In fact, without that law, you can't operate in the spiritual realm at all. It's not even possible. "And without faith it is impossible to please Him, for he who comes to God must believe that He is and that He is a rewarder of those who seek Him" (Hebrews 11:6). Without executing biblical authority through personal responsibility aligned in your faith, you simply can't do business with God. It's impossible.

Once you get clear on what God wants and is willing to do for you in light of what you need, you can talk to God about it through prayer and take the necessary action steps in light of that truth. That's called living in expectation. It's making decisions based on what you know God has already done while you wait on Him to bring it about. Much of what you may be wrestling with or struggling to overcome as a single, God has already taken care of. He's already provided the way out, in, over, around, or through. He's just waiting on you to tap into His provision by exercising your rightful authority in the name of Jesus Christ.

When faith is absent, you can limit God. Now, you don't limit His power. But you do limit the delivery of that power to you. Faith, in and of itself, is the most important element in living as a successful kingdom single. God is not going to force the victorious single life on you. Like Joshua, you have to go get it based on what God has revealed to you through His Word and the confirmation of His Spirit. That is, unless you're satisfied with living a half-victorious kind of life.

Every single must ask the question: What has God asked me to believe and to ask Him for at this season in my life? And what actions, thoughts, or words must I take in faith to back up that belief?

Kingdom single, God longs to move your mountains. Lord knows, He certainly can. He's just waiting on you to ask Him, in faith, and then do what He says in the process.

Forgiveness

There is one more condition Christ gave the disciples when He told them how to move the mountains in their lives. In addition to faith, they were to add forgiveness. Immediately after telling the disciples about the powerful nature of faith, Jesus followed it up with these words: "Whenever you stand praying, forgive, if you have anything against anyone, so that your Father who is in heaven will also forgive you your transgressions. [But if you do not forgive, neither will your Father who is in heaven forgive your transgressions]" (Mark 11:25-26).

What does forgiveness have to do with your overcoming challenges in your life and exercising kingdom authority? Everything. First of all, unforgiveness creates a barrier between you and God. God is holy and cannot dwell in the presence of sin (Isaiah 59:2). But more than that, God values forgiveness so greatly that He offered up His own sinless Son, Jesus Christ, to die for our sins so He could forgive us.

In light of all that God has forgiven you and me, when we choose not to forgive someone else, we're placing ourselves on a higher level than even God (Matthew 18:21-35). He won't stand for that, and, as a result, the mountains in your life will remain standing right where they are. Forgiveness in and of itself is an act of faith, because it means trusting that the wrong done to you will either be vindicated by God, reversed, or healed by Him.

What's more, holding on to grudges and unforgiveness brings about ruin in your own life. It keeps you stuck, distracted, and in a perpetual state of surviving rather than thriving. I'm sure you are not surprised when I say that one of the greatest ways Satan keeps you from moving the mountains in your life is by keeping you looking at your past. While the enemy says, "You can't, because of the damage that has been done!" God says, "You can, in spite of what has been done" (see Jeremiah 29:11). God will never *define* you by your past, but the enemy will try to *confine* you by it.

The first principle to understand when it comes to forgiveness is to never let your yesterday keep you from your tomorrow. You are to learn from yesterday, just don't live in it. The Israelites struggled with this very thing after escaping from a 430-year domination by the Egyptians.

The Israelites had left Egypt, but Egypt had not left them. As they sent the spies into the Promised Land, they stood on the precipice of a glorious tomorrow. But because they chose to focus on the pain and pleasures of their past rather than overcoming the challenges in their tomorrow, they did not move forward. As a result, they were forced to wander in the wilderness for forty years so that God could disconnect them from their past.

Many singles cannot get to their tomorrows because they're still carrying a connection to, and baggage from, their past. This connection, especially when it's unhealthily tied to a person through bitterness or regret, prevents people from moving forward in developing themselves and forming new relationships. Far too often it becomes nearly impossible to take that needed step into their future because they can't even get through today.

Does this sound familiar to you at all? You may have been delivered from the offense, or offenses, mistakes, sins, regrets, relationships, and more, but they hold just as much weight over you today because they haven't yet been delivered from you. In other words, you may no longer be tangibly tied to the situations or people in your past, but the remnants of their impact remain attached to you.

Maybe you feel you should be further in your life by now. Maybe you feel you should have been married by now, or further in your career, dating relationship, family, finances, or even your emotional and spiritual well-being. But instead, you keep looking back. You keep saying, "What if," "Why," "But," "I shouldn't have," and everything else that can be said about yesterday.

You fear that what happened to you has so shattered or altered you that you will never regain the hope and freedom you once knew. You fear that someone else has messed you up too much, stolen your future or your innocence. Or that your own poor and sinful choices have delayed you from being where you want to be, or even "disqualified" you from your dreams. You may even feel you no longer deserve a bright tomorrow; you haven't forgiven yourself for choices you may have made in periods of anguish, immaturity, or desperation to simply cope.

I know that sounds harsh, but so many people stop seeking to move the mountains in their lives or even hoping for marriage because they're too consumed with their regrets. They choose to settle in their dating relationships or settle for never marrying because they don't feel they deserve better.

Kingdom single, I understand that yesterday is real. Yesterday's choices are real. I'm not saying yesterday isn't real. What I *am* saying is that you need to stop looking at it so much that you miss out on today, and thus dim the light of your tomorrow.

When someone has sinned against you, or you have committed sins that you regret, it's like a wound or a cut on your soul. If that wound is left untreated, it will fester, and bacteria will begin to grow. For example, if you got a nasty cut on your arm but didn't clean it or care for it, in time that wound would start to ooze with pus, and the pain would increase. So much so that even if you were to go about your day with your wound nicely covered by your shirt, and someone accidentally brushed up against it, you would jolt in pain and lash out at the person.

Unforgiveness has the same effect. When the wounds in your soul are left untreated, they fester and rot. They create residual pain in other areas of your life. Then even the slightest brush by someone else—even if the person meant nothing wrong—can cause you to react in ways you normally wouldn't or in ways that the other person can't understand.

One word we often use for these unintended "brushes" against a wound is *triggers*. Triggers do more harm on dating relationships than most anything else. When you or someone you love gets triggered on a pain point from the past, you or they may lash out, accuse, blame, cry, or say and do things you or they later regret. Triggers may even cause someone to sabotage a dating relationship before it has a chance to grow into something deep. Triggers are overreactions, as the pain from the past resulting from unforgiveness is brought forward into what may have been just a slight nudge in the present. When these overreactions occur, the other person is caught off guard and often offended by this, and trust diminishes in the relationship.

If or when you carry this into a marriage, devastation will occur. Scripture tells us, "There are three things that make the earth tremble—no, four it cannot endure: a slave who becomes a king, an overbearing fool who prospers, a bitter woman who finally gets a husband . . ." (Proverbs 30:21–23, NLT).

To remove bitterness from your heart and position yourself in an emotionally healthy space so you don't find these triggers negatively affecting your current relationships, you must forgive.

You must forgive others. You must forgive yourself. And, yes, you must even "forgive" your disappointment with God if you harbor anger at Him for seemingly allowing negative situations in your life. You must treat your wounds, allow them to heal, and then take your focus off your scars by putting your focus onto the present moment. Keep your mind aware in the present day—living one day at a time, not in the past—and you will discover the freedom you need.

> Surrender *simply means accepting—accepting that despite what may have happened in the past, God was not caught off guard.*

One way to do this is through surrender. *Surrender* simply means accepting—accepting that despite what may have happened in the past, God was not caught off guard. He can redeem it for good, if you let Him. Life feels like trigonometry sometimes, doesn't it? It just gets so complicated, and nothing seems to add up. But if you'll start with the foundational truth that God is sovereign and He providentially arranges things to accomplish His goal, then you'll have laid a foundation through which to view, understand, and accept the complexities of life's pain that comes your way.

In God's providential connecting of things in your life, He either has caused all things or allowed them to happen (Romans 8:28). That is not to confuse God with endorsing sin. God hates sin and cannot sin Himself. But even though He doesn't endorse sin, He will use the sin that comes from a fallen humanity to accomplish His purposes. God will never let your pain go to waste. It will only go to waste when you choose to embrace unforgiveness, bitterness, regret, and doubt rather than forgiveness and faith.

The struggles you've faced that have given birth to unforgiveness are not some random chaotic mess, as they may have appeared. God has a purpose for what He allows. Unfortunately, we often miss that purpose because we get too focused on the pain.

However, through the power of forgiveness, you can dignify your difficulties by unearthing the miracle God is taking you to through the mess. Like the pain an athlete feels by working out in order to gain greater strength, trials and troubles do the same for a believer, if you allow them.

Keep in mind, forgiveness is a decision. It is not first and foremost an emotion. It's not about how you're feeling at any given moment, but rather about the choice you've made to *no longer credit an offense or blame against an offender*, even if that offender was yourself. Biblical forgiveness is the decision to no longer seek to enact vengeance. God said, "Vengeance is mine, I will repay" (Hebrews 10:30; see also Deuteronomy 32:35). It also involves releasing that person from a debt owed, as well as from the blame he or she deserves due to an infraction or sin committed against you.

The best biblical defense for this definition of forgiveness is found in 1 Corinthians 13, where we read about love. In verse 5 we discover that love "does not keep a record of wrongs" (HCSB). That doesn't mean love justifies the wrong, because to justify it incorrectly would not be love. Instead, that would be enablement. Neither does it mean that love ignores the wrong, excuses it, or pretends it didn't happen. Like a spouse of an alcoholic who continues to clean up the mess from last night's disaster, ignoring a wrong only provides the opportunity for the offense (the sin) to continue.

Love means you don't keep a record of the wrong. This is similar to how God forgives us. He doesn't forget the sin, but He no longer holds the offense against our account. We are not held in debt to Him to pay off something we're unable to pay.

I don't know what it is that you need to forgive. It could be a number of things. Maybe it was something that happened to you when you were young. Maybe it was an abusive mate. Perhaps you were forsaken, neglected, abandoned, or misused. You could have been played, maybe even more than once. Or wrongly demoted. Maybe you were even let go. Whatever it was—whether it was other people's sin or your own—remaining in the midst of the mess of unforgiveness will only distract you from summiting your destiny.

My friend, it's time to forgive. And with that forgiveness, coupled with faith, it's time to move the mountains in your life and exercise the kingdom authority afforded to you as a kingdom single.

5

THE CONTENTMENT OF SINGLES

Perpetual singleness was never a part of God's original intention for most people. The Dominion Covenant is clear that God's purpose for all mankind included male and female marriages that multiplied the human race through childbearing. This, then, resulted in the worldwide expansion of His kingdom agenda (Genesis 1:26-28).

However, when sin entered the human race, with it came selfishness, abuse, immorality, abandonment, divorce, desertion, and death. All these things and more contribute to an overabundance of singleness. This reality has caused even committed Christian singles to have to live a portion or all their lives with unfulfilled desires, dreams, and passions. The fact that a single is saved does not automatically cancel or override the physical, emotional, and relational desires common to humanity.

What, then, is God's means for addressing this reality? The answer is God's grace gift of contentment. While contentment does not cancel the loss that Christian singles experience, it does give them the spiritual capacity to be okay in spite of it.

This is why the apostle Paul could write of simultaneously having lack and yet also contentment. Contentment didn't remove the lack in his life, but it transcended it in such a way that he could successfully handle the unfulfilled areas. Contentment enabled Paul to avoid becoming ensnared in the pull of that which would take him off course for God's best in his life.

A lack of contentment leaves a person open to a wide array of temptations, as well as their resultant consequences. While the single life is often punctuated with gaps and with loss, living it in a spirit of discontent can lead to an even greater degree of loss in many ways.

The story is told of a dog that was wandering around its owner's yard one day. The dog was carrying a large bone in its mouth. When the dog came to the edge of a pond, it looked into the water and saw a reflection of what it thought was an even larger dog with what seemed to be an even larger bone. Wanting the bigger bone, the dog immediately opened its mouth to go after it. Yet in the process, the bone in its mouth dropped into the water and quickly sank to the bottom, out of reach. Not only did the dog fail to get the illusion of the larger bone, but it also lost the one it had been enjoying all along.

> *Discontent has a way of causing us to lose what we already have in an effort to gain what often does not even exist.*

Discontent has a way of causing us to lose what we already have in an effort to gain what often does not even exist.

How many Christian singles have given up their well-being, peace of mind, health, hope, and hearts in an effort to go after the illusion of intimacy and wholeness without the bonds of marriage or without entering into the right kind of kingdom marriage? Far too many have done so, based on the flow of tears in my office while counseling single after single for more than four decades now. Far too many wind up with less of themselves while searching for that someone to complete them, failing to realize that they are to be complete in who they are alone. Marriage, then, becomes an added bonus.

Not being satisfied with what you already have is the quickest path to losing it.

Friend, learning the virtue and value of contentment will save you from a lifetime of regret, remorse, and shame. Not only that, but it will also position you to experience happiness, favor, and increase. This is because not only does cultivating a spirit of contentment protect you from loss, but it also brings you great gain. First Timothy 6:6 tells us plainly, "But godliness actually is a means of great gain when accompanied by contentment." Godliness (the act of aligning your choices underneath God's overarching rule) coupled with contentment produces growth, productivity, satisfaction, and progress in your life.

Contentment is the secret to living as a successful kingdom single. Contentment doesn't mean you don't want something different. But it does mean you're going to be okay and at ease where you are right now until God provides it.

Coveting is the enemy of contentment. It is craving and pursuing something or someone that God has not yet legitimately provided. Coveting in Scripture is viewed as a sin of idolatry (Colossians 3:5). This is because it places what you want on a higher level than your love for God. Contentment (acceptance of and gratitude for what you currently have been given by God) is the antidote to the idolatrous sin of coveting.

Learning Contentment

But how do you get this valuable quality of contentment to work for your good? It's not as easy as asking for it, wanting it, or going somewhere to buy it. Rather, contentment is something you have to *learn*. In a sense, it's something you also have to *earn* through a myriad of life lessons aimed at instructing you on where to focus both your thoughts and desires. Paul gave us insight into how to obtain contentment when he wrote, "For I have *learned* to be content in whatever circumstances I am" (Philippians 4:11, italics mine).

Paul wasn't born with it. Neither were you. Neither was I. Just look at any infant, toddler, or teenager and you'll quickly recognize that contentment doesn't come as part of our DNA. In fact, this very absence of contentment is what Satan exploited in the Garden in order to usher in the first failure of sin.

Eve had hundreds (if not thousands) of healthy, vibrant, strong, and fruit-filled trees surrounding her from which to choose to enjoy. Yet the snake drew her focus away from all of those and onto the one tree she could not have. Not only that, but he also reminded her that by eating of this forbidden tree, she would gain something else she did not possess: the ability to be "like God."

It didn't take much more than a simple appeal to Eve's discontent to drag her into a decision laced with dishonesty. It rarely takes much more for any of us as well, which is why the subject of contentment is so critical, not only for you as a single, but also for you if you were to one day be married. After all, discontent is the leading cause of divorce. People call it by other names, such as irreconcilable differences, an affair, or a mid-life crisis, but the root is always the same. The root is a lack of contentment.

> *True contentment is never based on your circumstances. Contentment rises above your circumstances.*

But Tony, you may say, if only this would change or that would change or I could find a romantic partner or get a new job or get out of debt or . . . and so on. I can fill in the blanks because I've heard it all before. And I understand the heart behind what you may be saying or thinking. Yet keep in mind that true contentment is never based on your circumstances. Contentment rises above your circumstances. Let's take a closer look at Paul, who gave us one of the greatest examples of what contentment authentically is as a single believer.

When Paul wrote the letter to the church at Philippi, he was under house arrest. He'd been jailed for no legitimate reason, chained by lock and key. No doubt he was given scraps for food, if anything at all. Yet if you were to read through his entire letter to the church at Philippi, you would see a recurring theme. Over and over again, you would read words like, "Rejoice in the Lord," "God of peace," and "I thank my God."

How could those be the words of a man unjustly imprisoned, cut off from his friends, and lacking all the creature comforts our world has to offer? Those were Paul's words because Paul had learned the difficult but critical lesson of contentment. We read,

> Rejoice in the Lord always; again I will say, rejoice! Let your gentle spirit be known to all men. The Lord is near. Be anxious for nothing, but in everything by prayer and supplication with thanksgiving let your requests be made known to God. And the peace of God, which surpasses all comprehension, will guard your hearts and your minds in Christ Jesus.
>
> Finally, brethren, whatever is true, whatever is honorable, whatever is right, whatever is pure, whatever is lovely, whatever is of good repute, if there is any excellence and if anything worthy of praise, dwell on these things. The things you have learned and received and heard and seen in me, practice these things, and the God of peace will be with you.
>
> But I rejoiced in the Lord greatly, that now at last you have revived your concern for me; indeed, you were concerned before, but you lacked opportunity. Not that I speak from want, for I have *learned* to be content in whatever circumstances I am. I know how to get along with humble means, and I also know how to live in

prosperity; in any and every circumstance I have *learned* the secret of being filled and going hungry, both of having abundance and suffering need. I can do all things through Him who strengthens me. (Philippians 4:4-13, italics mine)

Paul's circumstances ought to have provoked him into fussing, cussing, and complaining. But instead, he spent his time reminding others to think on positive things and to rejoice, practice excellence, and learn the secret of living with either abundance or need. So what is Paul's secret that he learned?

The first thing he learned is that contentment is not automatic. It's learned. Paul had to learn contentment, not just flip a switch and turn it on. You don't just wake up content, nor do you get contentment simply because you pray for it. Have you ever prayed, "Lord, make me content in my singleness," and then wound up more miserable after the prayer than you were before? This is because contentment is not a spiritual gift—it's a character quality forged in the fires of circumstances. In order to learn something, you have to be exposed to the information you need to learn. You don't just learn something out of thin air.

So what information do you need to be exposed to in order to learn contentment as a kingdom single? Thankfully Paul shares that information with each of us. The way God teaches us contentment is through circumstances that bring about discontent. You have to face situations that force you to discover the value and choice of contentment.

Let me give you an example from Paul's life. In 2 Corinthians 12:7 we read, "Because of the surpassing greatness of the revelations, for this reason, to keep me from exalting myself, there was given me a thorn in the flesh, a messenger of Satan to torment me—to keep me from exalting myself!"

Paul acknowledges in this verse that God allowed Satan to send the particular problem he was facing. We don't know what it was, but we do know it challenged him deeply. We also know that God wasn't answering his prayer for a change in his painful circumstances. But in the next few verses, we discover the secret Paul spoke of regarding contentment:

> Concerning this I implored the Lord three times that it might leave me. And He has said to me, "My grace is sufficient for you, for power is perfected in weakness." Most gladly, therefore, I will rather boast about my weaknesses, so that the power of Christ may dwell in me. Therefore I am well content with weaknesses, with insults, with distresses, with persecutions, with difficulties, for Christ's sake; for when I am weak, then I am strong. (2 Corinthians 12:8-10)

It is God's grace, and God's strength in the midst of his tormenting circumstances, that Paul learned to apply to his own personal pain. God teaches us contentment by giving us circumstances where He doesn't immediately address our prayer request directly. He will even allow the devil to bring about the problem, if need be. But when there's a spiritual need that supersedes the physical need, God seeks to address the long-term spiritual need first. Remember, His thoughts are not like our thoughts. He is after our holistic growth and development, not merely our temporary delights.

God is after our holistic growth and development, not merely our temporary delights.

Friend, when your circumstances are not in your favor and you have to lean on God in a way that you wouldn't normally, He becomes more prominent to you. You discover that depending on God's strength in your periods of weakness allows you to be content despite the ups and downs, the highs and lows, that life routinely brings your way. Paul activated his dependence by glorifying God in appealing to His grace in the midst of his discontent. This brought him the stability and power he needed to deal with his negative circumstances (2 Corinthians 12:9). So, as you deal with your struggles, glorify God in the midst of them, and see His power meet you in your weakness.

My son Anthony really struggled with asthma as he was growing up. We would take him to the doctor for epinephrine shots when he would have an asthma attack. I'll never forget taking him into the doctor's office and the doctor entering with a large needle to put in his skin. I would see the needle, but Anthony always saw something else. That's because the doctor would also be carrying a lollipop. As Anthony started licking the lollipop, the doctor would then insert the needle. At first, Anthony would cry and yell because it hurt. He was in pain. He was struggling. But as tears rolled down his cheeks, his eyes would begin to focus again on the sweetness of the lollipop.

Now, don't misunderstand me; the lollipop didn't stop the pain. Rather, the sweetness shifted the focus off the pain until the pain eventually went away.

I'm not trying to be super-spiritual by emphasizing this area of contentment. I know it hurts when you're by yourself and you don't want to be. I know it hurts when other people have relationships that are going somewhere and you don't. I know it hurts and it may cause you to cry when you see couples enjoying each other around the holidays. I know it hurts if you've been abused, misused, or abandoned. I understand that. But Paul is trying to remind us that by focusing on God and His strength, by looking to Jesus Christ and the sweetness of His grace, you will discover that He is enough to reduce the impact of your pain and your attention on it. Just as God used Paul's pain to address a spiritual issue in his life, so also God allows weaknesses in us in order to take us to the next level of spiritual development.

Working in Our Circumstances

Whether Paul was enjoying abundance or doing without, whether he was winning or losing, he learned how to be content by navigating the process of these changes. Contentment must be learned, and that will require going through some experiences you may not want to go through. God teaches us contentment by allowing or creating changes in our circumstances, even (or especially) when those changes are not positive, and then instructing us through the outcomes of our responses, whether negative or positive.

The definition of contentment is to be at ease and satisfied regardless of what's happening around you or to you. As a single, that means living in a spirit of contentment even without the romantic partner you may long for. Or it could mean allowing your dating relationship to develop over an extended period rather than rushing to a level well beyond what singleness calls for. It also may mean letting go of that person you need to let go of. As my daughter Chrystal says, "Sometimes you have to let go of what's killing you, even if it's killing you to let go." Contentment gives you the emotional stability and security to walk away from a toxic relationship without regret.

As long as your emotional well-being is tied to your circumstances or to another person (or lack thereof), it remains temporary. Emotions can go up, down, and all around like a roller coaster because you haven't learned not to allow the situation, conversation, or relationship to dictate your ease, sense of satisfaction, happiness, and peace.

What constant and even drastic circumstantial changes in our lives, work, and relationships cause us to do (if we allow them to teach us) is to take our eyes off the changing seasons and place our focus instead on the unchanging Lord. Through this, we can learn the art of distancing our emotional well-being from our circumstances and other people. When you discover how to do this through practice, you will also discover how to make life choices from a position of strength rather than one of need. And we all know what happens when we make choices from a position of need, right?

Consider the simple illustration of grocery shopping on an empty stomach versus grocery shopping when you're full. How different are your carts going to look in those two scenarios? If you're like most people, the cart when you're hungry is going to be filled to overflowing, probably with way too many unhealthy, snack-type foods that you don't really even need. They just look good to you at the moment because you're hungry. Yet the cart you fill when you're not hungry will probably resemble something more along the lines of your actual grocery list or meal-prep ingredients.

Now consider the different results that might come about by searching for a romantic partner when you haven't discovered the gift of contentment versus when you have. I probably don't need to go into all the details about how those outcomes would be dissimilar for most people. You may have even personally experienced this already. If you're not operating from a foundation of surrender and contentment, you will be more willing to go further than you should, settle for less than you ought, and search in places where you never would have considered looking for someone before.

Friend, giving yourself the opportunity to make your decisions (and relationship choices) wisely, out of a contented and surrendered heart, mind, and spirit, is one of the most certain ways to ensure you will live as a victorious kingdom single. The key is found in Matthew 6:33, which we looked at earlier. You must seek first God's kingdom (God's rule over every area of your life) and His righteousness (God's standard of right and wrong); then He will take care of the rest. The point is that this commitment must precede all other priorities in your life for you to experience God addressing you at your point of need. While surrender does not guarantee God will give you a mate, it does guarantee you will experience your completeness and have your needs met as a kingdom single.

God's Providence

Paul also gives us two attributes of God that you must focus on if you're going to learn contentment in the midst of your struggles. The secrets we've been looking at are tied not only to your commitment to God first in your life, but also directly to your understanding of and focus on the providence of God. Providence simply refers to God's intentional arrangement of things beforehand for the fulfillment of His purposes. This includes the timing of open doors, closed doors, opportunities, people, places, plans, and more. Providence is God working things out behind the scenes with His invisible hand, like the great orchestrator He actually is. The only reason Paul was being attacked by the devil was that God allowed it. And God allowed it because of the purpose He had for Paul's life and to address a spiritual challenge he was dealing with (2 Corinthians 12:7).

Providence is God working things out behind the scenes with His invisible hand, like the great orchestrator He actually is.

There are two words that ought never to be spoken by a believer. These are *chance* and *luck*. The reason you should never say them is that they make it seem as if chance is controlling things or fate is running the show. In all actuality, God is in control, working things out and maneuvering the minutia of our lives so that all roads converge at the perfect time into what is known as your destiny.

The life of Joseph is a perfect example of God's providential hand in the ups and downs of a single man. His brothers sold him into slavery, but later he rose in Potiphar's household to a position of prestige. Yet he was later falsely accused of rape, only to be imprisoned and presumably forgotten. What's worse is that when he interpreted a fellow prisoner's dream, and that prisoner got released from prison, that other man failed to say anything on Joseph's behalf.

So for two very long years (doesn't time seem to go by a lot slower when you're alone?), Joseph waited in isolation until the opportunity came when he was called upon by Pharaoh himself. Going on to interpret Pharaoh's dream, Joseph found himself lifted from the pit to the prison to the palace, where God used him to save not only the Egyptian people from certain death, but also the neighboring nations, including Joseph's own family.

There's no greater statement on the providence of God than that said by Joseph himself in Genesis 50:20, where he told his brothers who had at one time betrayed him, "As for you, you meant evil against me, but God meant it for good in order to bring about this present result, to preserve many people alive."

Joseph was able to say this confidently because he knew that God Himself had been in, over, arranging, guiding, and providentially carrying out His plan in Joseph's life all along. The secret to his success during his years as a single man was clearly stated by Stephen in Acts 7. Joseph's secret was that the Lord was with him (verse 9).

Joseph married after his release from prison, and his wife gave birth to two sons. The meaning of his boys' names is enlightening. One was named Manasseh, which means, "God has caused me to forget all my toil and pain." The other was Ephraim, meaning "God has made me fruitful." Those two names sum up a kingdom perspective of letting go of the loss and disappointment life sometimes serves up on God's path to purpose, and embracing the fruitfulness of the calling He has created you to fulfill.

An important element to point out about Joseph as a kingdom single man is that even though he was handsome, buff, and enjoying success in the upward mobility of his career, he still refused to respond to the sexual advances of a woman. His commitment to his God overrode his libido (Genesis 39:6-9). Wisdom informed his decisions, not his hormones. This should be the goal of every single Christian man.

While Joseph gives us insight into a kingdom single man, Ruth does the same as a kingdom single woman. When her husband died, her mother-in-law, Naomi, faced a bleak future without much hope for security or food. Naomi had just lost both of her sons and needed to return to her home country. However, her sons had married women from another ethnic group, and expecting them to go with her now to a foreign land would be unthinkable. Urging them to stay, since they were young and could find other husbands among their own people, Naomi determined to set out on her own.

That's when Ruth made a spiritual decision to go with Naomi in order to place Naomi's needs above her own. Yes, she could have made a logical decision based on her own physical needs and desire to be married, as did her sister-in-law who stayed. Ruth would certainly have been able to find a husband among her own people and not risk a life of deprivation and loneliness. But Ruth's commitment to her faith and family superseded her commitment to herself. She made a kingdom decision, not merely a humanly convenient one. She chose to pursue God's kingdom over pursuing marriage. She said, "Do not urge me to leave you or turn back from following you; for where you go, I will go, and where you lodge, I will lodge. Your people shall be my people, and your God, my God" (Ruth 1:16).

She received this favor because she made a decision where she could not see the solution in advance.

As a result of Ruth's commitment, she walked straight into the providential hand of God, who not only connected her with her future husband, Boaz, while she served Naomi by gleaning leftover food in the fields, but also blessed her by opening the way for her and Boaz to marry (Ruth 4:1-10). Ruth would go on to give birth to a son named Obed, who later became the father of Jesse, who became the father of David, the king. In surrendering in love to the needs of those around her, Ruth was raised by God to the position of royalty. She received this favor because she made a decision where she could not see the solution in advance. All she knew was that her mother-in-law's people would be her people, and their God would be her God. She made a faith decision and as a result became a mother in the lineage of the Lord Jesus Christ (Matthew 1:5).

That's what providence can do!

God's providence is greater than any wisdom, logic, or maneuvering we may try to do on our own. He knows just how to take the seemingly unconnected events in our lives and weave them together when we pursue His highest rule (the rule of love, Matthew 22:36-40) as our compass.

And, friend, He can do the same for you.

Yes, it may feel as if God is trying to take you from point A to point Z in a zigzag across the Sahara and then the Serengeti, and it may seem that your life resembles a roller coaster of sorts. But in the process of the ups, downs, and sideways, God *is* seeking to teach you to trust His hand. When you learn to trust Him in spite of what you see, you will no longer need to try to buy your contentment, eat it, drink it, hook up with somebody for it, or even chase it. Your contentment will come as a result of knowing that He has a plan, and He means it for good in order to bring about His intended result.

God's Power

But not only did Paul have a focus on the *providence* of God, he also had a focus on the *power* of God. Paul discovered that grace has batteries. God's sufficient grace provided him with increasing strength to deal with his unchanging situation. And with that power came greater contentment (2 Corinthians 12:10). We discover this key aspect in verse 13 of the passage we looked at earlier in Philippians 4: "I can do all things through Him who strengthens me."

Now, I have a feeling that you may be like most everyone else who absolutely loves to quote this verse. But what many people fail to realize is that this ever-popular Scripture is tied to the subject of contentment. It's not just a general out-there-pie-in-the-sky promise. No, this passage refers to the infusion of strength that Paul receives from God in order to be content in situations where his own stamina and willpower can't go any further. Runners call this the second wind.

I used to run ten miles at times when I was younger, and, if you run, you know that you reach a place on the journey where you simply don't think your body can take one more step. Yet if you push yourself past that place, there is this jolt that infuses you with strength you didn't know you had. It's the second wind. And that's what Paul meant by this passage: When he was at his absolute lowest point and couldn't bear to bear up under any more, that's when God enabled him to remain steadfast, immovable, and always abounding, because God strengthened him through divine power, giving him a second wind. Thus Paul learned to be content even when he was weary.

One of the secrets to remaining steadfast is found through surrender. We all know what it means to surrender. It means to give in, to cry "uncle," or to offer up. In Romans 12:1, Paul says about our surrender, "Therefore I urge you, brethren, by the mercies of God, to present your bodies a living and holy sacrifice, acceptable to God, which is your spiritual service of worship."

Paul says that God wants you to present your body to Him. That's another way of saying "present your life to God," because anything you do is going to include not only your physical body, but also your mind and soul. The surrender found in this passage comes in the word *sacrifice*, which is a picture of an Old Testament sacrifice. When the priests sacrificed a lamb, they didn't just put its head or its legs on the altar. Rather, they placed the lamb's entire body on the altar. And when the lamb was slain, they didn't just take its body; that lamb gave its life.

In fact, when you look throughout Scripture, you'll find that whenever God wanted to do something special, He required a sacrifice first. Something had to be presented to demonstrate that the worshiper was both sincere and acting based on God's standard of holiness. That's why the sacrifice was called *holy*.

The great blessing we have today is that God wants living sacrifices instead of dead ones. Because Christ died as the once-for-all sacrifice for sin, we don't have to bring a lamb to offer for our sins—or forfeit our own lives. But that doesn't mean we have nothing to offer God that He wants. We learn in Romans 12:1 that God wants us to give ourselves fully to Him. This is the "spiritual service of worship" He wants from every single.

God's call to surrender is based on what He has done for us, as Paul explained in the first eleven chapters of the book of Romans. Here is a quick overview. In chapters 1–3, God says there is no one righteous; we've all sinned and fallen short of His glory. At the end of chapter 3, we read that God made a way by which sinful people can become righteous—through the sacrifice of Jesus on the cross. Romans 4 says we get this righteousness by faith in Christ's finished work, and we also get the benefits that come with salvation (Romans 5).

Romans 6–7 says that even though we're saved, we're still going to struggle with sin because we live in the flesh. But Romans 8 teaches that God has given us the Holy Spirit to overcome the flesh so we can live in spiritual victory. Chapters 9–11 explain that in Christ, God has given to us what He hasn't given yet to His people, Israel. Then Paul comes to Romans 12:1 and says, "Therefore," because of the high price paid for our salvation, God wants you to give all of you to all of Him. Nothing less is "acceptable to God."

Many singles want to give God just a little here and a little there. But He wants the whole body, the whole life. He's asking for surrender, which the Bible calls a "holy" act. The word *holy* in the Bible means something special, unique, set apart, in a class by itself, as opposed to something common.

You may have an illustration of this right there in your home. You probably have a set of "common" and "unholy" dishes that you use every day. Unholy dishes are the dirty dishes in the sink. Common dishes are the ones that you use daily out of the kitchen cupboard. They're not special. But then you have that set of dishes and stemware in the dining room hutch that is "holy," set apart for very special occasions only.

God says, "I want My own special place in your life. I want you to set Me apart and treat Me as holy. That's why I want you to present your body to Me as a holy sacrifice. Don't treat Me as common or ordinary."

Romans 12:2 tells us how to give ourselves wholly to God as holy, living sacrifices.

Many singles want to give God just a little here and a little there. But He wants the whole body, the whole life.

This verse begins, "And do not be conformed to this world." The Greek word translated "conformed" was used of a potter making a clay vessel on his wheel. The potter had to apply pressure to shape the clay. He had to use force to squeeze that lump of clay into the pitcher or bowl he wanted to make. It's important to note that the potter used *external* pressure; he was pushing from the outside to force the clay to conform to his will.

Paul is saying, "Don't let the world squeeze and pressure you into what it wants you to look like as a single. Don't let cultural pressure or public opinion shape your attitudes and ideas." It's easy to define yourself by the world's standards of a single, or even by the church's. Unfortunately, that often leads to feelings of insignificance or lack. Rather, God wants you to live by His standard of royalty, rule, and purpose.

After presenting the negative in Romans 12:2, Paul states the positive: "But be transformed by the renewing of your mind." "Transformed" in Greek is a word from which we get the English word *metamorphosis*. There's a big difference between this and the word *conformed*. Instead of outside pressure changing something, *transformed* refers to change that comes from within. A butterfly changes from within, completely transforming itself from a caterpillar to something beautiful.

Now here is where religion can get us in trouble. We can, even with good intention, make the mistake of trying to transform ourselves through actions, applying the same external pressure as the world. So we become worldly trying to become spiritual. The main way we do this is by coming up with all kinds of rules to govern our lives. If you've been in church very long, you know what I'm talking about: "If you really want to be a holy single, then don't go there, don't watch this, don't read the other, don't wear makeup or any adornment, and don't associate with that person."

The word for this is *legalism*, which is a misuse of the concept of law. The reason Jesus had to die on the cross was that none of us could live up to God's holy law. So why would we want to put ourselves back under law? The main reason is that we think it gives us a way to gauge our spirituality.

But if the mind doesn't change, then real change does not occur and we resort to sin management rather than real spiritual transformation. Real change comes when our motive for doing or not doing something transforms from "I have to" to "I want to." This frame of reference is completely different from the external pressure of legalism.

While the world is screaming at you, the Spirit speaks in a still, soft voice.

This leads us to a final point from Romans 12:1-2, the motivation to let God transform our minds. Most of us need an incentive to change. Well, God hasn't left us without a reason. It's at the end of verse 2: "So that you may prove what the will of God is, that which is good and acceptable and perfect." Our motivation is experiencing God's involvement in our lives at a level we've never known before.

The payoff for your refusal to be molded by the world and your surrender to God is that you get to "prove," or see, God at work in your life in such a way that He will express His perfect will—His complete purpose for your life—for you, to you, in you, and through you. This is something you will see only on a limited basis if the world is your dictator and you are saying *yes* to it and *no* to God.

So the question you have to ask yourself is whether you want to discover true contentment and experience the fullness of God's will and purpose for your life as a single. If you do, you need to listen to the Holy Spirit, because while the world is screaming at you, the Spirit speaks in a still, soft voice. Too many believers can't hear Him because they're listening to the world screaming at them. People say, "Why doesn't God speak to me?"

He *is* speaking; they just aren't listening.

As I write this chapter, our region of the world has been hit hard by fires on the West Coast, hurricanes in the Southern states, and an earthquake in Mexico. Chaos and confusion scream loudly all around us. It reminds me of an all-important passage found in 1 Kings 19:11-13, which says of the prophet Elijah,

> A great and strong wind was rending the mountains and breaking in pieces the rocks before the LORD; but the LORD was not in the wind. And after the wind an earthquake, but the LORD was not in the earthquake. After the earthquake a fire, but the LORD was not in the fire; and after the fire a sound of a gentle blowing. When Elijah heard it, he wrapped his face in his mantle and went out and stood in the entrance of the cave. And behold, a voice came to him.

Sometimes God will speak loudly. But often you'll need to learn how to listen beyond the raging roar of distractions, disappointments, demands, and desires. You'll need to listen for the still, small, gentle voice of the One whose power and providence are the only things that can usher you straight into your rightful rule and position.

Listen to Him. He knows what He's doing. He knows what He's preparing you for. He knows where He's taking you. And when you get used to hearing His voice and experiencing His grace, you'll have learned the secret of spiritual contentment as a kingdom single.

PART II

THE
CHALLENGES
OF A
KINGDOM
SINGLE

6

WINNING THE
SPIRITUAL BATTLE

If you've ever watched professional wrestling, it's basically entertainment. It's not a real battle; it's for pleasure watching. The winners have been preselected and predetermined. Yet even though they've been chosen for victory, they still have to fight to get the "W."

It's interesting that the eventual winner will often look as if he's being totally defeated, destroyed, and even disembodied when, all of a sudden, power comes out of nowhere to reverse the match. Because the victory has been prearranged, it can take place in the midst of a crisis and an enormous conflict.

The reality is that God has declared you, as a kingdom single, to be more than a conqueror. Victory has already been won for you. You're not fighting *for* victory; you're fighting *from* victory. Yet even so, there are still battles to be fought and things to be overcome. The speed at which you usher in your victory largely depends on how you face those fights.

One of the most victorious Christians ever to live, who was also a kingdom single, is the apostle Paul. We've looked at much of what he had to say as the basis for this book. Paul could speak eloquently on nearly any subject. He faced trials and difficulties with the vigor and vitality of a kingdom man. Yet Paul still had his struggles. He had his times of crisis, and how he chose to approach those times will give you insight on how to approach those times in your own life.

Struggles can come in all shapes and sizes. It could be an addiction to pornography or gambling. It could be codependency. It might be an emotional affair with a married person. It could be a propensity toward promiscuity, alcohol, too much spending, or any number of things. Struggles and crises lead us into addictions and challenges that are often difficult to overcome. So whatever your greatest struggle is, as we look at how Paul faced his own, insert yours into the equation, because what he has to say applies to you and how you can overcome the pull of the flesh and live victoriously in the Spirit.

In Romans 7, Paul lays out his struggle in a number of verses:

For we know that the Law is spiritual, but I am of flesh, sold into bondage to sin. (Romans 7:14)

For what I am doing, I do not understand; for I am not practicing what I would like to do, but I am doing the very thing I hate. (Romans 7:15)

So now, no longer am I the one doing it, but sin which dwells in me. (Romans 7:17)

But if I am doing the very thing I do not want, I am no longer the one doing it, but sin which dwells in me. (Romans 7:20)

Through these verses and more, Paul is being authentic and vulnerable in explaining his battle with his flesh and temptations. While he (and we) received a new nature, our sinful flesh still battles to please itself. The flesh is that unredeemed humanity we all have that seeks to satisfy itself independently of God. Men, the fact that Paul had to battle and find spiritual victory over his flesh as a single man ought to encourage you to do the same. Single men, like the apostle Paul, must work to "discipline my body and make it my slave" (1 Corinthians 9:27).

Disciplining the Flesh

If you don't discipline your flesh, your flesh will rule. What's worse, Paul tells us that the flesh actually feeds off the law. In Romans 7:11 he says, "For sin, taking an opportunity through the commandment, deceived me and through it killed me." Essentially, the Old Testament Mosaic law actually provoked a greater desire to break the commandments than to keep them. And while Paul desired in his spirit to obey God, he desired in his flesh to disobey God. Sound familiar? It's a schizophrenic kind of crisis that everyone faces at some point, if not in many points in life. It's the battle of the flesh.

We all face it. Some of us are just better at covering it up than others. I call it wearing spiritual Spanx. You know what Spanx are: They're something you wear that make you appear better off than you actually are. They're camouflage of sorts that hide the ugly reality underneath. When people live with spiritual Spanx, they appear more holy than they really are or declare themselves to be. They may easily be living in defeat while appearing to be victorious.

Those in that state may not be interested in hearing what Paul has to say about how to overcome the flesh. But if you're aware of your deficiencies, you will, because Paul came completely clean and admitted to what he could not get rid of on his own. In fact, he called himself a "wretched man" (Romans 7:24). This is a picture of a single, Christian man struggling with his unredeemed humanity.

Paul admitted to his wretched state because the flesh is unredeemable. You can hide it, cover it, and manage it, but you'll never be able to redeem it. In other words, you cannot make your flesh become spiritual. It's like how we all have fat and muscle, and you can lose fat and increase muscle, but you cannot turn fat into muscle. Those are two very different realities. You have to address both in order to get both the way God wants them to be.

Paul discovered it wasn't possible to whip his flesh into obedience. It was not possible to live in a state of sin management, promising to do better, wishing to do better, or following twelve steps to do better. The only way to overcome sin and the flesh is spiritual transformation—reducing the influence and presence of the flesh while strengthening and increasing the influence of the Spirit.

Daily, ongoing victory as a kingdom single through crisis, temptation, and struggle is achieved only through the Spirit. Paul gives us a peek into this at the end of Romans chapter 7 and as he begins chapter 8, where we read,

> Thanks be to God through Jesus Christ our Lord! So then, on the one hand I myself with my mind am serving the law of God, but on the other, with my flesh the law of sin. Therefore there is now no condemnation for those who are in Christ Jesus. For the law of the Spirit of life in Christ Jesus has set you free from the law of sin and of death. For what the Law could not do, weak as it was through the flesh, God did: sending His own Son in the likeness of sinful flesh and as an offering for sin, He condemned sin in the flesh, so that the requirement of the Law might be fulfilled in us, who do not walk according to the flesh but according to the Spirit. (Romans 7:25–8:4)

The law is law. There's no overcoming the law of sin and death simply because you decide to do so. Like the law of gravity that you cannot outwit or simply determine to beat, you won't be able to beat the law of sin ruling in the flesh. It will trick you, tempt you, lure you, and beat you every single time. But what Paul tells us in this passage is that there's another law at play that can override the law of sin. It's the law of the Spirit who lives within you.

When an airplane flies, it overrides the law of gravity. The law of gravity doesn't cease to exist. Rather, the airplane applies a greater, stronger law called the law of aerodynamics that overrules the impact gravity has on the plane. Similarly, God sets you free by giving you a law to override your flesh. By living according to this law, you have the power to overcome.

However, just as an airplane has to apply a certain speed and thrust and lift in order to enact the law of aerodynamics, there are things we need to do to enact the law of the Spirit within us. Paul tells us what these are in Romans 8:5-6: "For those who are according to the flesh set their minds on the things of the flesh, but those who are according to the Spirit, the things of the Spirit. For the mind set on the flesh is death, but the mind set on the Spirit is life and peace."

Let me give you a passage that will help this make more sense. It's found in Galatians 5: "But I say, walk by the Spirit, and you will not carry out the desire of the flesh. For the flesh sets its desire against the Spirit, and the Spirit against the flesh; for these are in opposition to one another, so that you may not do the things that you please. But if you are led by the Spirit, you are not under the Law" (verses 16-18). Paul informs us clearly through these verses that the secret to living a life free from the control of the flesh is to "walk by the Spirit." If and when you do that, you will not fulfill the desires of the flesh.

> *Paul informs us clearly through these verses that the secret to living a life free from the control of the flesh is to "walk by the Spirit."*

That could sound too simple, though, so let me put it another way.

What Paul doesn't say is to stop fulfilling the desires of the flesh so that you can walk in the Spirit. No, that's called Backwards Christian Soldiers. Rather, Paul states that if you walk in the Spirit, the resultant effect is no longer living out the desires of the flesh.

Keep in mind, he doesn't say you will no longer have those desires. That's not the case at all. I run into numbers of believers in counseling sessions who feel guilt or shame for having flesh-based desires. But the flesh is always going to want to do what the flesh wants to do. The desire may never disappear, but what will disappear is the actual living out of that desire. The problem is that we often equate the desire to the action. But God makes a distinction between the two. Not carrying out the action is what results from walking in the Spirit. The Spirit gives you the power to override what's inside. Thus, even though the flesh may be urging you on over and over again, because you are now functioning with the Spirit, you have the capacity to overcome.

Have you ever been at an airport and come across one of those moving sidewalks? When you get on a moving sidewalk, you're still supposed to walk. The benefit is that there is something beneath you that causes your walk to move that much farther ahead with a lot less effort. It's not that you stand there and stop walking. If you do that, you'll actually move slower than if you were to walk at your own pace. A moving sidewalk is there to assist you in getting where you need to go more quickly than you could have on your own.

God tells us that if you will simply walk in, or by, the Spirit, the Spirit will take you further in your spiritual victory and power than you ever could have on your own. The Spirit will enable you to have an override button to deny the flesh the fulfillment of its desires.

So stop trying to get your flesh to do something it was never designed to do, because the flesh can only sin. There is no such thing as victory in flesh management. Promising to do better will not cut it. Rather, transitioning your thoughts to the Spirit's thoughts, and walking in close proximity to Him and in Him, will provide the supernatural override necessary to make victory real. Only in aligning your thoughts with those of the Holy Spirit through prayer, coupled with dependence and obedience, will you discover the power that comes through walking in the Spirit. As you move forward spiritually, the Holy Spirit will lead you to where your heavenly Father wants you to go.

Victory in the Crisis

Your victory and your peace come from where you choose to set your mind. They depend on where you decide to allow your thoughts to go. They depend on what you allow into your mind by way of entertainment, music, and conversation. They depend on whether you make time to meditate on God's Word and His attributes and your personal life decisions. They depend on whether you rebuke and cast down thoughts that are contrary to God's truth. The mind set on the Spirit, which is God's way of thinking on a matter, is your key to victory as a kingdom single.

It is unfortunate today that many Christian singles are simply out of their minds. By that I mean that their minds are not functioning rightly. They're living with an improper or distorted mind-set and then wondering why their souls aren't working well and why they're struggling so much. But the answer to that is simple, because the mind is to the soul what the brain is to the body—the centerpiece of function.

If a person's brain fails to operate as it should, that person's body will reflect it immediately. There's simply no way around the cause-and-effect connection of the brain to the body. Similarly, when our minds get off track from a kingdom-based mind-set, our choices, thoughts, and ultimately our souls suffer the consequences. If you have a messed-up, carnal mind, you'll have a messed-up soul. And if you have a messed-up soul, you'll have a messed-up body, because your body functions based on the dictates of your soul.

Since the mind is the key with which you unlock data for the soul, how your mind is oriented and how it not only interfaces with but also filters and applies that data will determine your well-being and progress as a kingdom single.

In the book of Colossians, Paul gives us clear and explicit insight into where and how our minds are to operate as believers in Christ. We read,

> Therefore if you have been raised up with Christ, keep seeking the
> things above, where Christ is, seated at the right hand of God. Set
> your mind on the things above, not on the things that are on earth.
> (Colossians 3:1-2)

In this passage, Paul instructs us that we are to adopt a mind-set that stems from where Jesus is located. We are to seek things above with Christ, but also from the vantage point of Christ, who is seated at the right hand of God the Father.

Now, before you brush over this passage too quickly—perhaps because you've read it before or have heard it taught on—give me a moment to unpack these principles fully. Because if you can truly grasp and apply the truths found here, it will save you a tremendous amount of heartache, headache, and hopelessness further down the road as a single.

The first point for your attention is that Jesus is sitting down. Why is that important? Because when Jesus rose from the grave, He ascended to heaven and was seated at the right hand of the Father (Mark 16:19). He was positioned there on purpose. And the reason He could be seated was that His work had been finished. The work He had come to Earth to accomplish had been accomplished in full. Therefore, your victory has already been won.

Second, Paul gives us the next mental point of reference when we continue reading in verse 3 of Colossians 3, "For you have died and your life is hidden with Christ in God." This paints a picture of who you are and where you also are seated.

In other words, you are also seated with Christ in heavenly places (Ephesians 2:6). Not only does Christ complete you, but He is to be the sum total of your point of reference as well. His mind-set is to be your mind-set. As Paul wrote elsewhere, "But we have the mind of Christ" (1 Corinthians 2:16).

> *Christ's thoughts are not to be some of your thoughts. It's not His opinion versus everybody else's opinions.*

Christ's thoughts are not to be *some* of your thoughts. It's not His opinion versus everybody else's opinions. Or His opinion mixed in with yours. This isn't "group think," where everyone gets to voice a view and the majority wins. No, your entire mental makeup is to be fully, unequivocally couched in Christ. To operate according to a kingdom-based mind-set is to think, discern, and do all according to the mind of Christ. It is to fully live out your life under the comprehensive rule of God.

So how do you make this work in pragmatic, day-to-day terms? Because the world's mind-set, your friends' mind-set, and even your own flesh-based mind-set are what seem the most real to you. I know and I understand, because that seems the most real to me, too. Our fleshly perspective is rooted in a physical world we understand and know, in a world that we can touch, smell, taste, hear, and feel. Yet while the world may be very, very *real* to us, it may also be very, very wrong.

Living life from a spiritual mind-set requires breaking free from your comfort zone and going beyond your physical understanding. But if you choose to do it, it will be the difference between living a victorious life as a single or a defeated one.

Living this way will involve three distinct components: Faith about the facts, your function in light of the facts, and your feelings rooted in faith.

How Does This Relate?

How does this relate to being a kingdom single? When my kids were growing up, there was a popular television show called *The Facts of Life*. It revolved around some high school students as they came to grips with learning and understanding life. Now, this was a show rooted in a secular worldview, so I can't say they always got it right, but we do have a source of information that does get it right each and every time. It's called "The Facts of God," and it's the Bible. The facts of God that we learn through His revealed Word usher us into an understanding of truth. Truth is God's mind on a matter—what He says about it and what we therefore ought to believe about it. Essentially, it is having God's point of view.

Yet how are we to discern God's point of view? We do this through studying His revealed will and His character and attributes in Scripture, His Word. We read in Psalm 119:160, "The sum of Your word is truth, and every one of Your righteous ordinances is everlasting." And while God may not tell you specifically to take this job or that one, to move to Dallas or Hawaii, or whom to marry, He does give you principles in His Word that the Holy Spirit will use to guide you in the application of His truth to your personal situation.

Let me illustrate this in a practical way with a problem some of you may struggle with, or have struggled with in the past—swearing. This doesn't have a lot to do with being single per se, but it will get the point across without running the risk of getting lost in a myriad of emotions often tied to singleness.

When it comes to the issue of swearing, we begin by discovering God's point of view on it. We read in Ephesians 4:29-30, "Let no unwholesome word proceed from your mouth, but only such a word as is good for edification according to the need of the moment, so that it will give grace to those who hear. Do not grieve the Holy Spirit of God, by whom you were sealed for the day of redemption."

And as we read further into Paul's letter to the church at Colossae, it says,

> When Christ, who is our life, is revealed, then you also will be revealed with Him in glory. Therefore consider the members of your earthly body as dead to immorality, impurity, passion, evil desire, and greed, which amounts to idolatry. For it is because of these things that the wrath of God will come upon the sons of disobedience, and in them you also once walked, when you were living in them. But now you also, put them all aside: anger, wrath, malice, slander, and abusive speech from your mouth. (Colossians 3:4-8)

In verse 8, Paul lists different kinds of sins. Two of these sins are "slander" and "abusive speech." Now, regardless of how you personally feel about what God says, or what your friends have to say about what God says, His truth is clearly written out for us on this use of our mouths and words.

So if you were struggling with swearing, the first thing you would need to do would be to align your mind-set with the fact that God says you should not use profanity. Abusive speech ought not to be a part of your normal way of speaking.

Then, second, when you're tempted to swear, you must develop the habit of asking Jesus to respond for you. That's what "walking by the Spirit" truly is. When you ask Jesus to respond for you, then what He would want to have come out of your mouth begins to be the dominant response. Walking in the Spirit is so important, because the Holy Spirit does not want to be grieved by speech that hinders His work in your life. Therefore, bringing your speech into the context of His presence and developing the habit of Christ controlling your tongue is essential.

Not only are you to avoid swearing, but God's Word tells us in other places that you are to use your words to lift up others and edify them. For example, Colossians 4:6 says, "Let your speech always be with grace, as though seasoned with salt, so that you will know how you should respond to each person." Let me outline it for you in this way:

The first step is to ascertain the facts (God's truth on the matter).

The second step is to ask Jesus to respond for you in the power of the Spirit.

The third step is to align your function within the boundaries of those facts.

The facts say that God gives you power to do all things, including controlling your tongue (Philippians 4:13). Not only does God not want you to use your mouth wrongly, but He also gives you the strength and discipline to obey Him. This requires operating out of the new mind-set and not from your flesh.

Let's make this even more practical. Let's say you have a tendency to swear when another driver cuts you off in traffic. If you live in Dallas as I do, I can understand this temptation! But even though it's a temptation, God's Word instructs you to use your mouth for edification and not for destruction. You know the facts even if your emotions still respond with anger and frustration.

God's Word instructs you to use your mouth for edification and not for destruction.

But here's the great thing about emotions. Emotions do not have intellect. Emotions simply respond. So while your emotions may be responding in such a way as to encourage you to swear at the driver who cut you off, your mind can override your emotions by setting a plan in place for when triggers like this occur. A plan may be a sticky note you leave on your dashboard with a Scripture to remind you to watch your mouth. Or it could be actively practicing speaking encouraging things about other drivers before and when no challenges exist.

You see, in swearing, you allowed the behavior to become a habit. You've allowed your emotions to instruct your mind rather than the other way around. In order to break a habit, you must now engage your mind on how to overcome your emotions.

The best and most effective way to do that is when you're not in the middle of a triggering situation. That's why I suggest making it a practice to speak encouraging words about other drivers when things are going along well. As you continue in this habit, and as you carry it out over a period of days, weeks, and months, the old habit of swearing when cut off by a bad driver will seem more and more abnormal to you when the trigger occurs.

Of course there are other ways to approach this, and you may have one that works best with whatever challenges you're facing, but these are two practical ways to demonstrate that aligning your mind and your behavior with God's prescribed will needs to be intentional. The intentionality of writing the sticky note and placing it on the dashboard occurs before the trigger. So also does the intentionality of replacing negative words with positive ones about other drivers.

Paul emphasizes this in Colossians 3:10 by reminding us of the intentionality it takes to overcome temptation: "Put on the new self who is being renewed to a true knowledge according to the image of the One who created him." He tells us to put on the new self.

This is a function. When you choose to put something on, it's a decision you've made. Your emotions and your mouth will no longer dictate what you say. Instead, based on what Jesus has declared, you now have control over your mouth. But you have to decide to use that control, and you have to practice the use of that control in order to develop it into a new habit.

Putting on the New Self

Putting on your new self can be explained by comparing it to a situation where a person has just taken a shower. Now, it goes without saying (at least I hope it does) that after a person takes a shower and gets washed up, he or she puts on clean clothes. Surely, someone who has just showered won't put on the same dirty, grimy, sweaty, stinky clothes taken off before the shower. A person doesn't go through the whole process of getting yourself to smell well just to cancel it out by sticking on old, dirty clothes.

So when Paul refers to putting on the new self, he's reminding you and me that we've been created new in Christ. To go back to the same choices and lifestyle decisions of the flesh that are normal and natural to our sin nature would not be commensurate with the cleansing Christ died to procure. Thus, the question you ask yourself related to your speech is simply this: "Does my speech reflect the cleansed, new nature I possess in Christ?" If the answer is no, there needs to be a change in your function so that the answer becomes yes.

How does this relate to being a kingdom single? The same principle applies to all areas of navigating the single life. You're to find out God's truth (the mind of Christ) regarding any issue you're facing, whether it's the kind of character of the person you want to date, matters of sexual purity, how you choose to spend your time, where you're to find your value and worth, what God thinks of singleness, your purpose, your finances, and more. Then, after finding God's truth on the matter, you align your actions within the boundaries of that truth. It's there that you'll discover the freedom and favor the Father seeks to give you by operating from His vantage point and not your own.

Functioning from a mind-set that you are a new creation in Christ will then influence your feelings. Colossians 3:12-15 gives us the process of how this occurs:

So, as those who have been chosen of God, holy and beloved, put
on a heart of compassion, kindness, humility, gentleness and patience; bearing with one another, and forgiving each other, whoever
has a complaint against anyone; just as the Lord forgave you, so
also should you. Beyond all these things put on love, which is the
perfect bond of unity. Let the peace of Christ rule in your hearts,
to which indeed you were called in one body; and be thankful.

The peace of Christ is given to you, but notice that it comes after you
align your function with the rule of God through kindness, humility, gentleness, and love. You can't start with your feelings and then move to the
function. Yes, your feelings are real, but feelings don't have intellect. They
simply respond to the circumstances of life. It's only when you start with
the facts (the truth) and let them inform your function that you then get to
experience the good feeling, the peace of Christ, as it rules in your heart.
You begin in faith in order to get to the feelings. Your feelings are the ca-
boose, not the engine.

Now, I'm not saying you should deny your feelings. If you feel mad,
you're mad. Or if you feel sad, you're sad. If you feel lonely as a single, you're
lonely. But what I *am* saying is that God's Word teaches us that if you place
your faith in that Word and function according to His rule, He will change
your feelings and give you peace and calm where you were once frantic and
worried. Why? Because you will be operating from a different point of
view.

Suppose you think you've forgotten to pay a bill, and you're worried the
power company is going to turn off your electricity. But then, as you're
walking around nervous about everything, you run across a receipt or a
cancelled check that shows you paid it. Once you realize the bill has been
paid, your feelings will adjust. The previous feeling was real—yes. It was
just wrong because it wasn't based on fact.

You don't start to feel differently because you focus on changing your feelings. If you're lonely as a single, focusing on not feeling lonely isn't going to change that. It'll actually make it worse, since you'll be thinking about it all the time! But when you focus instead on the fact that God promises to never leave you or forsake you (Deuteronomy 31:6), and that He will meet all your needs, even those lonely needs (Philippians 4:19), you will begin to function from a mind-set of wholeness and security rather than emotional scarcity and lack.

You will stop running to distraction after distraction, looking for ways to salve your soul, and instead live in the confidence that God has a plan for you, and that it's a good plan. You'll stop having to shop, date, drink, or go further in giving your body than you should in an attempt to meet a need God Himself has already promised to meet—if you will but align your mind-set and actions in Christ under His rule. And trust that His providential hand will provide exactly what you need—and who you need—when His timing is right.

Paul's ability to live victoriously as a kingdom single completely depended on where he chose to place his thoughts. Likewise, the key to your victory as a single is guarding your mind—protecting it, preserving it, and intentionally focusing on the truth of God's Word rather than the lies of Satan and the chatter of the world. When you do that, you will experience the peace that passes understanding, and you will truly know the power of the Spirit within you.

7

GETTING HELP
FROM HEAVEN

I've spent the bulk of our time together in the heart of this book trying to open your mind to another viewpoint on singleness, especially the positives that God has provided you through this unique season or role. I've intentionally done this because in my decades of counseling singles, I have seen that the positives are overlooked the most. And while there are many positives to being single, and some who are even called to this status for life, I am not naïve to the pain that is also attached to it.

You may be saying right now, "That's great, Tony. Those are awesome things I can focus on. But I still really, really, really long to be married." And if that's you, please know that you're completely normal. Scripture even speaks of a single woman who went and mourned the fact that she was to remain single her entire life. Essentially, she mourned her status of virginity (Judges 11). So if that's you, and your desire for a mate continues to dominate your thoughts and emotions, and you don't know what to do with your dissatisfaction, I want to direct your attention to a few women in the Bible who have shown us what can be done.

But before we do, I want to remind you of our definition of a kingdom single. A kingdom single is *an unmarried Christian who is committed to fully and freely maximizing his or her completeness under the rule of God and the lordship of Jesus Christ.* That's the foundation. Once that's in place, and you still find yourself strongly desiring a mate, then move forward in pursuing one with the principles found in this chapter and the next.

Throwing the Challenge Flag

There are those times in life when you want to act like a coach in a football game and throw a red flag out on God. For those reading who are not football people, a red flag is a "challenge flag." You throw the flag out when you believe the referee has made a mistake. It's when you think he has made a bad call, he didn't call the play right, so you challenge his call in order for it to be reviewed and, hopefully, reversed.

> *There are those times when we believe God has made a mistake. Of course, we would never say that publicly, but we feel it.*

Truth be told, there are many times when we want to do just that with God. We want Him to reverse what He has allowed or change the path we've been placed on due to the previous call. There are those times when we believe God has made a mistake. Of course, we would never say that publicly, but we feel it. We feel that God has done us wrong somehow, and that the call He made simply wasn't fair.

Perhaps you feel it's not fair that you're unmarried or that your mate walked out on you; maybe you lost your mate and now you're a widow or widower. Perhaps you feel your job situation isn't fair or your finances are wrong, and you just want to throw the red flag out on God. Your life is not where you want it to be. Despite all your best efforts at keeping a positive outlook, your chin up, and your feet moving forward, at the end of the day—when it's just you sitting there alone—you believe that God has made a bad call along the way.

There's a story in John chapter 11 where two single women feel exactly the same way. Their names are Martha and Mary. Martha, Mary, and their brother, Lazarus, were very close with Jesus when He lived on Earth. In fact, it was Mary who had anointed the Lord with ointment and wiped His feet with her hair. Their bond was true, and they felt they could count on Him. Yet when Lazarus fell sick, Jesus opted not to come to their home right away.

Martha and Mary had done what good Christian women ought to do when they're struggling. They called on Jesus. Yet despite doing everything they should, Jesus stayed away. One day turned into two, two turned into three, and so on. Before they knew it, their brother had died. No doubt, these two women wanted to throw the challenge flag out on God. Why didn't the miracle maker come to their home? Didn't they mean anything to Him?

To make matters worse, when Jesus heard of Lazarus' death, He offered no comforting words. "And I am glad for your sakes that I was not there," Jesus said in reference to Lazarus' dying a few days before. Wait a minute now! Martha and Mary were full of tears, and Jesus responded by telling those around Him that He's glad He wasn't there? Challenge flag time, definitely.

Yet when Jesus arrived, He answered Martha's challenge with His own. In the face of her accusations on how His delay led to her brother's untimely death, Jesus challenged her to believe. He challenged her to place her faith more deeply in Him than it had ever been.

In fact, the reason He was glad He had delayed was so that His power could be made manifest in an even greater way than ever before. We read, "This He said, and after that He said to them, 'Our friend Lazarus has fallen asleep; but I go, so that I may awaken him out of sleep'" (John 11:11).

He had plans to turn the situation around all along. Martha and Mary just didn't know it. They had focused on what they could see rather than on what they believed.

Friend, if all you see is what you see, you will never see all there is to be seen.

In the next few moments, Jesus spoke with both Martha and Mary and became moved by their pain. While He was glad for the opportunity to demonstrate His power so that many would believe, His heart broke under the weight of His friends' sorrow, and He wept (John 11:35). After composing Himself, He asked Martha to have the stone removed over the entrance to Lazarus' tomb. She then reminded Him of the basics of mortuary science. Surely her brother's body would be decomposing by this point. Removing the stone was the last thing anyone wanted to do. Yet Jesus urged her to believe Him and have her actions reflect that belief.

I don't know what it was that convinced her; it could have been their long history or the depth of their relationship. Whatever it was, Martha did what most people would have never done. She took a step of faith in the midst of unbearable pain. And that step was rewarded as Jesus performed the greatest miracle of that day—He called forth Lazarus from the tomb.

Just as God raised Lazarus from his grave, so also God can raise up people today from their sense of loss and bring them back to life as kingdom men and women. Single reader, God has a plan that includes both the ordinary and extraordinary things in life. But His plan is always timed to His agenda, not yours. However, you can delay His plan if you choose to remain in your disappointment for things that have not gone according to your plans. If Martha or Mary had chosen to argue, sulk, and simply ignore Jesus' request to move the stone, they might have never gotten their brother back.

Don't let this life pass without your discovering God's extraordinary gifts and redemption for you because you choose to remain so disappointed with Him that you skip moving the stones He asks you to move. You will never discover God's secret will until you obey His revealed will.

What is the stone you need to move? Is it a person you need to cut ties with? Is it sexual activity you need to stop participating in? Is it a pursuit of your career or calling with more intentionality and passion? Whatever the stone is, it's your job to move it.

And keep in mind, the task may not make sense from a human perspective. I understand that when something or someone dies, there's a loss of hope. Things look as if they're over, dead. Some of you have dreams that have died. Others have had a previous marriage or relationship that died. And your hope is gone. But do you know why Jesus hung back and allowed Lazarus to die? He did so in order that those around Him could experience a resurrection through a miracle. The only way you can ever get a resurrection in your life is when something dies first—when it's over as far as humanity is concerned.

When you consider your present situation and see that the natural world is not offering the solution you desire, could it be that God is delaying because He wants you to see what a resurrection looks like? Never let a stone block your miracle. Never let human wisdom and rationale block your miracle. Never let what your friends think or say block your miracle. Cry out to Jesus and to Him alone. Then, when you hear from Him, do what He says to do. He is the source of your resurrection.

Earlier in Scripture, in 2 Kings chapter 4, we read about another death. This was the death of a good man who feared the Lord and had a family for whom he provided. Yet after his death, his widow and children were left in a dire predicament. In fact, the creditors had decided to come and take the children away as slaves. Not only had this woman lost her husband and experienced the grief that comes with that, but now she faced losing her children as well. This is when the prophet Elisha entered the equation and brought heaven to bear on Earth.

When she cried out to Elisha, he gave her a solution. He instructed her to take all that she had in her home, which was a jar of oil, and then go to her neighbors and borrow their vessels to pour her oil into. That instruction carried as much common sense as Jesus telling Martha to move the stone away from her brother's four-day-old corpse.

But faith doesn't rest on a foundation of common sense. Faith rests on the foundation of God Himself. So the woman did as the prophet said, and not only did she fill all her neighbors' jars full of oil, but she had enough left over for herself and her family. She sold the oil to her neighbors, paid off her debt, and had plenty for her and her sons to live on.

Both women cried out to God in the face of an unsolvable situation. And both women were asked to do something completely contrary to what anyone would have thought to do.

Notice the correlation between the two stories. Both women cried out to God in the face of an unsolvable situation. And both women were asked to do something completely contrary to what anyone would have thought to do. Both women also obeyed. And both women got a reversal in their situation.

Hope Deferred

But what if your situation or season has seemed to go on longer than those of these women in the biblical stories? After all, both situations involved disasters that had occurred in a relatively short time. Often it's easier to cry out to God in the immediacy of an urgent moment. But what if you've been single for a decade now, or even two, and the issues you face as a result go on and on, with no end in sight? It's in those times that it may be more difficult to cry out to God or to keep crying out to Him.

Proverbs 13:12 says, "Hope deferred makes the heart sick." When unchanged circumstances go on for so long, they can literally make you feel sick about your season. Now, I know there are many contented singles, and this chapter won't apply to everyone. But I also know there are many singles who simply feel that going on another day, week, month, year, or even decade as a single is a letdown. It's a "hope deferred." And when hope becomes deferred, it's easy to give up, hang your head, and simply mope through life rather than embracing it or facing it with joy.

What should a kingdom single do when carrying a heart burdened by a season that's gone on too long? A glimpse into the life of another woman named Hannah will give us great insight into how to cry out to God in the midst of a long drought within yourself and your own needs.

When we come across Hannah in the book of 1 Samuel, we find a woman who was not doing well at all. Yes, she was married, but the principles of her story apply to singles who are looking to become married as well. While Hannah wasn't looking to become married, she was looking for a "someone" in her life. Hannah desperately wanted to be a mother; she wanted a child.

Married to a man at a time in biblical culture when multiple wives were the norm, Hannah found herself empty in the area that mattered most to women in that society—family. Her husband's other wife had already borne him children, "but Hannah had no children" (1 Samuel 1:2).

We know that Hannah's husband loved her deeply despite her lack, because we read that he "would give [her] a double portion, for he loved Hannah, but the LORD had closed her womb" (1 Samuel 1:5). Yet even with her husband's love, Hannah suffered because children during this time secured a future for their parents and a legacy. Children were a critical and essential part of life, especially as parents aged. Hannah wanted nothing more than to have a child.

Hannah's rival enjoyed witnessing her defeat over and over each year. Her rival was a bully who taunted Hannah regularly. We read, "Her rival, however, would provoke her bitterly to irritate her, because the LORD had closed her womb. It happened year after year, as often as she went up to the house of the LORD, she would provoke her; so she [Hannah] wept and would not eat" (1 Samuel 1:6-7).

Hannah was in a lonely situation. Not only that, but this wasn't just a bad day or a bad holiday season. This loneliness, and reminders of her lack and loneliness, went on for years.

There's something about a prolonged crisis that drains hope even more completely. It's like sitting in an emergency room and waiting for your name to be called, but watching everyone else go in one by one. While you're in pain, confusion, and worry, time seems to slow to a crawl. Yet those around you don't even seem to care. You become tired, weak, and scared. If you aren't careful, your feelings will suck the life out of your faith.

Hannah had a big problem in her day. She couldn't get pregnant. If a doctor were to examine her, he would have chalked it up to something biologically wrong. But as we saw in the earlier passages, Hannah's body had not betrayed her. Rather, the Lord had closed her womb. Hannah's issue wasn't physical at all. It was spiritual, just like so many of the issues we face today. The reason Hannah couldn't conceive was not due to some physiological malady, but it was God Himself blocking her conception. Now, if God has closed your womb, it doesn't matter which doctor you go to, because no doctor would have the ability to overrule God.

Similarly, many of the problems and the emptiness, barrenness, or complications you may face in your life as a single aren't as tied to the physical realm as they may appear. Because this is true, make sure that when you examine the struggles in your life, you don't merely judge what you're facing by what you can see. Instead, ask yourself if God has something to do with your inability to produce results, connect with others, find the right person, or discern your own areas of needed growth. Hannah's physical limitation and her emotional irritation by her rival had a reason, which God would reveal later. The trials and troubles you're facing right now in your single season, if allowed by God, might have a reason as well.

If you find yourself praying for a mate for a prolonged period and are getting nowhere, or so it seems, ask God to reveal what He's doing behind the scenes. Sometimes just understanding that there's a bigger kingdom plan in play can provide you with the insight you need during times of desperation. It can guide you toward what you can do next, like Hannah.

Despite not getting a child for years as she had wanted, Hannah models for us what we're to do regarding requests that God seems to delay on. Year after year, Hannah went up to the temple to pray. Her emptiness hadn't stopped her from going to church, bowing her head, or seeking the spiritual. She hung in there waiting for her change to come. But then one day, it looked as if it all became too much for Hannah, and she broke down in desperation and wept.

It's always okay to cry. It's okay to reach that point where you admit you cannot go any further apart from God's intervening hand.

It's always okay to cry. It's okay to reach that point where you admit you cannot go any further apart from God's intervening hand. Life is hard. Setbacks, breakups, and unmet expectations leave us all weary when they hit. Hannah had suffered more than she could handle by then, and the Scripture tells us she "wept bitterly" (1 Samuel 1:10).

Friend, when you weep bitterly, that means you're wailing. That's not just when tears are flowing down your face. Wailing means you've reached the end of your rope. It's the deep pain that knows no comfort. It's those times when even a hug or a kind word from someone would do little good. Weeping bitterly usually comes when we have lost all hope for change.

It's in those desperate times that desperate measures—things we normally wouldn't do—come to mind. Just as they did with Hannah. She made a decision at that moment. She struck a bargain. She would give her child back to God if He would give her a child. She made a deal—a vow, a promise, an oath. We read, "O LORD of hosts, if You will indeed look on the affliction of Your maidservant and remember me, and not forget Your maidservant, but will give Your maidservant a son, then I will give him to the LORD all the days of his life, and a razor shall never come on his head" (1 Samuel 1:11).

Hannah had been praying to get pregnant for years, but this time her prayer took on a whole new intensity. Her desire for a child was so strong that she was willing to let go of the thing she wanted most if she could but have him for a while.

Serving God

This brings us to a very important point regarding praying for a mate. In Hannah's prayer, she let God know what He would gain by answering her. She made it about Him. She focused on how His kingdom would be advanced and His name glorified. That's a heart in alignment under God.

For singles, you'll want to ask: How would having a mate better help you to be effective in serving God? In what way could you possibly help this potential mate serve the Lord more fully than he or she can as a single? You should be developing good answers to these questions. He has placed each of us here on Earth as representatives of His kingdom, with a divine mission to fulfill—expanding His rule on earth and bringing Him glory. Why would He want to give you a mate who will only limit you (or that potential mate) in living out the purpose He's given to both of you?

Far too often, we don't even consider how God will benefit when we ask for things. We're paying so much attention to what we want that we forget the fundamental truth that this world and our lives were created for God's purposes. He has a plan. He has a kingdom agenda. If you want your requests granted, then discover how those answers will benefit God and His kingdom. If they don't, you may have to acknowledge that you're asking with selfish motives rather than out of a heart that loves God first (Luke 10:27). We're commanded to put God first in our lives and with our lives

(Matthew 6:33), yet frequently we don't even consider Him, His desires, or His will in our requests and longings.

Ask yourself these questions regarding praying for a mate:

Is what I'm praying for going to benefit others?

Does my request, if granted, bring glory to God?

How will this request advance God's kingdom agenda on Earth?

Will the answer to my prayer equip me to serve God more fully?

These are the types of questions to ask as you seek to align your heart's motivation with God's will. Hannah wanted a son, yes. But she knew first and foremost that her life was ultimately about God and His rule. So she made a strategic decision with regard to her prayer need. She aligned it under God's hand. She literally chose to give Him the literal manifestation of her heart's desire. And, remember, this was no small desire. Hannah longed for a child as much as was humanly possible.

Even her demeanor reflected a woman distressed in grief as she made her vow to the Lord. The priest nearby as Hannah prayed at the temple thought she was drunk. We know this because he said, "How long will you make yourself drunk? Put away your wine from you" (1 Samuel 1:14).

Hannah was a mess. But she didn't care what people saw. Sometimes troubles can get so deep that the things we used to concern ourselves with don't matter anymore. Have you ever been in a place like that? Hannah pled before the Lord, making her vow in such a way that those around her thought she had lost her mind. But hearing the priest's concern and knowing his position before the Lord, she replied as someone would who was in her right mind: "No, my lord, I am a woman oppressed in spirit; I have drunk neither wine nor strong drink, but I have poured out my soul before the Lord. Do not consider your maidservant as a worthless woman, for I have spoken until now out of my great concern and provocation" (1 Samuel 1:15-16).

The priest heard more than Hannah's words, he heard her heart. He believed her, blessed her, and told her that God would give her the child for whom she had asked. Scripture records that when Hannah heard what the priest had to say, she believed him and went on her way no longer sad. She had faith that her prayer—her vow—would be answered.

What happened next is often overlooked in the study of Hannah's life. Just two verses summarize it, but it reveals a lot about the ingredients of intentional prayer coupled with belief. For starters, we read that Hannah ate. She had been hurt for so long, not only by her barrenness but also by the taunting of her rival, that she had stopped eating for some time.

Yet with the news from the priest that her prayer would be answered, Hannah returned to a state of calm that enabled her appetite to come back. She began to feed her body and regain her strength.

Then, in the next verse, we discover that Hannah had relations with her husband—sexual intimacy. For couples who have tried to conceive year after year, the act of intimacy can become a reminder of loss and pain. It can turn from the joyous celebration it was intended to be into a task filled with emptiness and regret. It's beyond "Why bother?" to "I don't want to be reminded of what we never get." But Hannah and her husband didn't allow the years of barrenness to change their behavior. Upon word from the priest that she would conceive, Hannah and her husband acted in faith.

Acting in Faith

One of the mistakes we often make as we face the various trials and challenges in our lives is to become inactive. When the mountain seems too high to climb or too large to move, we sit back and leave it all for God to do, as we saw in our chapter on faith. Too often God is waiting on us while we think we're waiting on Him. He's waiting to see if we will carry out our actions of obedience, even in the face of the seemingly impossible. Had Hannah *not* had relations with her husband, she would never have gotten pregnant.

Hannah's pregnancy was much bigger than her. Your desire for a mate, and the answer to that prayer request, are much bigger than you. God has a plan to impact others through you, which is why He will often let you get to the point where you know it's He who brought something about. But that won't happen without action tied to your faith.

Too often God is waiting on us while we think we're waiting on Him.

Faith never implies lack of action. Faith is a participatory sport. It means acting as if God is telling the truth. Or as you will hear me say, *faith is acting like something is so even when it is not so in order that it might be so simply because God said so.*

Hannah did more than sit around and wait for God to send a stork with her special package. She acted on the truth that God was going to give her a son. And then, when He did, she fulfilled her vow and gave Samuel back to Him. We read,

> So the woman remained and nursed her son until she weaned him. Now when she had weaned him, she took him up with her, with a three-year-old bull and one ephah of flour and a jug of wine, and brought him to the house of the LORD in Shiloh, although the child was young. Then they slaughtered the bull, and brought the boy to Eli. She said, "Oh, my lord! As your soul lives, my lord, I am the woman who stood here beside you, praying to the LORD. For this boy I prayed, and the LORD has given me my petition which I asked of Him. So I have also dedicated him to the LORD; as long as he lives he is dedicated to the LORD." And he worshiped the LORD there. (1 Samuel 1:23-28)

There are occasions in life when God has a unique purpose to fulfill. Because of this, He will allow a rare delay or setback, or even a difficulty, to happen. God didn't respond to Hannah until she made her vow to give back the very thing she wanted most. But she wasn't willing to give up her son until she reached her point of desperation.

If the Lord has pushed the pause button on your request for a mate, don't give up. If He has delayed His answer, don't stop trusting. All that means is that He's driving you to a point of spiritual depth and experience with Him that goes beyond the norm. He wants to blow your mind with something—to have you see Him reveal something that's beyond the natural in order to accomplish a greater kingdom purpose. But far too often, you or I will not open our eyes or hearts to the depths of the spiritual until things get desperate.

Giving Our Desires to God

God had a special plan for Hannah's firstborn child, Samuel. Samuel would go on to be an instrumental prophet in the land of the Israelites, affecting both the present and future generations. Yet had Hannah not reached a period of utter despair, she may have held on to Samuel for her own gain.

Sometimes God asks us to let go of something for His sake that we would never let go of other than at a point of crisis. Isn't that what He made Abraham do? He asked Abraham to sacrifice his son—his only son through Sarah, the son whom he loved. When Abraham, in faith, gave his son to the Lord, God gave Abraham back his son.

Luke 6:38 is a powerful verse that we often fail to understand completely, but it directly applies to the fruitfulness and power of our prayers. It says, "Give, and *it* will be given to you. They will pour into your lap a good measure—pressed down, shaken together, and running over. For by your standard of measure *it* will be measured to you in return" (italics mine).

Notice the word *it* in that verse. That's a small but powerful word. Whatever you're asking God to give you, give *it* to Him. Whatever the substance of your prayers contains that you want God to do for you, change for you, fix for you, or whatever, see how and where the *it* can be given back to God or to others in His name. Hannah wanted a child, so she gave God a child. Abraham wanted his promise of legacy, so he gave God the son through whom that legacy would occur. Give the very *it* that you're seeking, and *it* will be given to you. God is good on His Word.

Are you relationally barren? Then give of yourself relationally to someone else in need, perhaps a shut-in or an elderly person at a group home. Are you financially struggling? Then by all means be generous to someone else in need—as generous as you can be.

When you step out in faith and give out of your lack to someone else, you're demonstrating that you believe God when, based on your circumstances, believing Him is the last thing you want to do. You're operating on faith even though you can't figure out how and when your solution will ever come.

Do you need answered prayer? Then seek to be the answer to someone else's. The standard of measure you give will be the standard of measure you'll receive in return, and then some. Bear in mind, God usually outgives us. Hannah didn't just give birth to Samuel. She got more than she asked for. In the next chapter of the book named after her son, we read that Hannah "conceived and gave birth to three sons and two daughters" (1 Samuel 2:21). Hannah got a houseful after all.

Do you need answered prayer? Then seek to be the answer to someone else's.

If you're struggling right now as a single and you don't know how much longer you can last, take heart. Allow yourself to go low, even to the point of weeping bitterly like Hannah, because it's at that point that you'll find the freedom to trust God fully. It's at that point you'll find the powerful tool called *surrender*. Surrender that which you think you need so desperately into His hands and providence. When you do, God will give you the strength to keep going in order to reach His perfect plan for your life. Give the very thing you want (companionship, support, leadership, and more) to someone else who needs it—perhaps another single, an elderly person, or a child who needs mentoring.

Surrender your *it* to God.

Surrender is the secret to answered prayer. It has opened more doors, and even wombs, than we realize. Surrender is letting go of your timing, your will, and even your intended purpose and trusting God in His.

A woman we read about in 1 Kings 17:9-24 illustrates this point so fully. Here was a single mother with a son to feed who had run out of the means by which to live. She was destitute. In fact, she had only enough oil and flour for one more meal. Yet God sent her a boarder, the prophet Elijah.

Notice that God told Elijah, "I have commanded [her] to provide for you" (1 Kings 17:9). So this woman was about to be confronted with the issue of obedience to God. And God will often ask you to give up the very thing you think you want or need most. That's what happened when Elijah came to this single woman and asked her for a meal. The widow told him her plight and that she was planning a last meal for herself and her son because of the famine (verse 12). She was saying, "I don't see any way out."

I have sat with single parents who have said the same thing. I think any single parent can understand how this woman must have felt. Her statement was not in conflict with God's desire for her, because at this point she was simply stating the reality. Her obedience hadn't been tested yet. She didn't have much, but Elijah asked for it anyway, because he knew what God was going to do.

This woman faced a big question, one that many single parents face today: Do I obey God even though I'm a single parent who has very little to offer? Or do I take the little I have and keep it for myself? She did have the promise of God to act on, for Elijah told her:

Do not fear; go, do as you have said, but make me a little bread cake from it first and bring it out to me, and afterward you may make one for yourself and for your son. For thus says the LORD God of Israel, "The bowl of flour shall not be exhausted, nor shall the jar of oil be empty, until the day that the LORD sends rain on the face of the earth." (1 Kings 17:13-14)

Here is the classic dilemma for singles who are longing for a mate, or for single parents trying to get by financially. Are you going to obey God and get His long-term blessing, or are you going to disobey Him in order to get a short-term fix? Many singles will settle for the latter because they have a hard time seeing with the eyes of faith.

This single widow could have said no to Elijah and eaten her last meal. But she had a heart that was open to the God of Israel, and she acted on His word, not on her situation. What God wants you and all of us to do is to learn to operate on His Word and not our circumstances.

The widow of Zarephath had a heart to obey God, and we read in 1 Kings 17:15-16 how God kept His promise made to her by Elijah. She and her son not only did not die, but they also "ate for many days." God kept her jar and bowl filled with enough flour and oil for each day's need. God gave her what she did not have enough of when she gave Him what little she did have.

Before you complain about what God isn't doing for you, or how lonely you are and how long you've been praying for a mate, your first question must be, *Am I doing what God told me to do?* Secondly, *Am I willing to give back to God what I want so deeply if He were to give it to me?*

When you're able to answer those two questions in a manner that's in alignment under God's kingdom rule in your life, you'll be positioned to receive your request.

8

THE POWER
OF INTIMACY

Jesus was the greatest single of all time. Single for the entirety of His life, He is the consummate role model for a kingdom single. As a single man, Jesus fully experienced every aspect of human life that every other human— and yes, every other single person—experiences. Even though Jesus was God in the flesh, He never used His deity to negate or override the reality of His humanity.

Jesus needed to physically grow (Luke 2:52). He got weary (John 4:6). He needed to sleep (Mark 4:38). He felt abandoned (Matthew 26:40). He was betrayed (Luke 22:34). He felt sorrow (Matthew 26:38). He experienced rejection (Mark 8:31). He cried (John 11:35). He faced satanic temptation (Matthew 4:1-10). He felt what it was like to be forsaken by man (John 16:32) and even by God (Matthew 27:46), wishing His Father would intervene and change His circumstances (Matthew 26:39).

Jesus experienced all this and more so that He could feel what it was like to be fully human (though without sin), so He could sympathize with you both in your humanity and in your singleness (Hebrews 4:15).

Jesus not only understands where you are, but He also feels where you are. And because He's perfect, He feels it at the highest possible level.

What, then, was the secret of Jesus' victory as a kingdom single, and how can His secret enable you as a kingdom single to be victorious and productive too? The answer is found in one word: *abiding*. It was Jesus' intimate connection with the heavenly Father that enabled Him to have the character necessary to live victoriously as a single man. What's more, He offers that same opportunity to every serious disciple of His, whether married or single (John 15:9-10).

This concept of a kingdom single's character is vividly explained in John 15 and is the key to your success as a kingdom single.

The Need for Fruit

When God wanted to provide an illustration and a word to explain what knowing Him fully would produce in the lives of believers, He used the concept of *fruit*. Fruit is God's spiritual reference to what our lives produce when our character reflects His. In fact, Galatians 5:22-24 speaks explicitly of this fruit when we read, "But the fruit of the Spirit is love, joy, peace, patience, kindness, goodness, faithfulness, gentleness, self-control; against such things there is no law. Now those who belong to Christ Jesus have crucified the flesh with its passions and desires."

In no other place in Scripture are the attributes of the character of God laid out so clearly. If you want to know the character of a kingdom single, just look at the results of a life belonging to Christ and filled by what the Holy Spirit produces.

Yet fruit refers to more than just our character. It also refers to what is produced for the benefit of others through us by His character reflected in us. God wants you to maximize your productivity *for* Him through your connection *to* Him.

In business, we would call this generating a healthy return on investment. In sports, it's known as a winning game or season. In music, it's a platinum album. And in your personal life, producing fruit means leveraging all at your disposal for the betterment of yourself and others and the glory of God. This even applies to what you choose to think and say: "Through Him then, let us continually offer up a sacrifice of praise to God, that is, the fruit of lips that give thanks to His name" (Hebrews 13:15).

For starters, fruit has three distinct characteristics: visibility, authenticity, and availability.

You've never seen or eaten invisible fruit. You've never gone shopping for invisible fruit. Fruit is always something you see. You can see an orange, pear, apple, banana, or whatever kind of fruit there is before you. Similarly, if your relationship with Jesus Christ produces results that aren't visible to others—or even to you—there's not much of a relationship there at all. Fruit is always visible.

Second, fruit always bears the character of the tree of which it is a part. You won't find pears on apple trees or oranges on pear trees. This is because fruit authentically replicates the nature of the tree from which it grows. When believers resemble anything other than the character and qualities of God, they are not relationally attached to God. Yes, they may be eternally saved through Christ's atonement on the cross, but their souls on Earth have neglected the process of being sanctified.

In your personal life, producing fruit means leveraging all at your disposal for the betterment of yourself and others and the glory of God.

For example, if you reflect the values of the culture, then the culture is the source you tap into. Or if it's a combination of culture, entertainment, self-interests, or even a social circle that is reflected in your thoughts, words, and actions, then those are the things to which you're attached. This is because fruit authentically resembles what it's attached to. Many singles are malfunctioning like an appliance that doesn't work correctly because they're letting the culture and not God define them.

Lastly, fruit never exists for itself. Fruit is always available for consumption by someone else. The only fruit you ever see eating itself is rotten fruit. Think about it: When fruit is rotten, it begins a process of eating away at its own existence, shriveling into only a shell of its once-wondrous beginnings. Fruit exists so that someone else can bite it, be nourished by it, enjoy it, and grow from it.

God desires for you as a kingdom single to bear much fruit. How do I know that? Because Jesus tells us in John 15:16,

> You did not choose Me but I chose you, and appointed you that
> you would go and bear fruit, and that your fruit would remain,
> so that whatever you ask of the Father in My name He may give
> to you.

You have been chosen to be productive. You have been appointed to maximize your potential. You have been created to nourish, give to, and delight others through the gifts, skills, time, and talent the Lord has placed in you. Your calling to live as a full-on, fire-breathing, sold-out, sanctified child of the King has nothing to do with your marital or relationship status. God isn't waiting until you're married for you to use your life to feed, equip, and strengthen others. He has a purpose for you, and that purpose belongs only to you. You are to bear fruit—fruit that will last. You're to leave a legacy. Yes, *you* as a kingdom single have a legacy to leave behind!

How to Produce Fruit

So how do you go about this process of bearing fruit as a believer in Christ, since it is what Jesus desires of you? Is there a special formula? Does it require an extreme amount of effort? Does it happen when you wake at a certain hour to pray, or when you cross off a list of things that you think will make you a successful kingdom single? Does it mean going to church whenever the doors are open or volunteering whenever someone is needed?

Actually, you may be surprised to discover that bearing fruit takes the right kind of effort. Track with me on this: Have you ever seen a pear or an apple struggling and straining to become a pear or an apple? Or how about grapes on a vine? No, you have never seen that, just as I have never seen that. This is because the simple act of abiding brings about the growth of the fruit. It's in your closeness to Christ that you create fruit both in and through your life.

Paul gives us insight into how our relationship with God determines our productivity for Him in Colossians 1:10: "So that you will walk in a manner worthy of the Lord, to please Him in all respects, bearing fruit in every good work and increasing in the knowledge of God." In this passage, there is a direct connection between bearing fruit and knowing God.

The Greek word for *knowledge* used in this verse is *epignosis*. It means "to have full knowledge of, to know." So far, so normal—right? To know God means you should read your Bible. Say a verse a day to keep the devil away. Go to church. Say a prayer. Take an online course on Scripture or theology. That's typically how we interpret what it means to know God. And that's also typically why so few of us truly live out the full manifestation of His fruit in and through our lives. This is because to *know* God goes much deeper than informational knowledge alone. It's not just about content. It's about so much more.

Let's travel back to the beginning of measured time to get a deeper glimpse into what it means to fully *know* someone, and what that knowing can produce. In Genesis, we read another instance of a word we translate as "knowing" when it says, "And Adam *knew* Eve his wife; and she conceived, and bare Cain, and said, I have gotten a man from the LORD" (Genesis 4:1, KJV, italics mine). The word translated into "knew" in this passage is the Hebrew word *yada*. *Yada* simply means "to know," "to know by experience," and "to perceive." When Adam knew Eve, it didn't mean he had information about her. No, he slept with her. In other words, there was a level of intimacy that produced fruit. It bore new life.

To know someone encompasses more than just knowing *about* someone. To truly know someone involves an engagement, interaction, intimacy, and understanding that go above and beyond cognitive realities. Have you ever seen a couple who have been married four or five decades, and it's as if each can finish the other's sentence before the other barely gets a word out? Or consider dancers who spend hours upon hours, days, weeks, and months practicing together. They know each other's moves, moods, and more simply through being close. They can anticipate the next step and know how to bring out the best in their dancing partner.

The best linebackers in the NFL are those who have worked so closely together that they can predict each other's moves simply through a shift in weight or a change in the placement of a hand. With crowds roaring and tensions high, these linebackers don't have time to talk to the other linebackers to find out what they're thinking. But those who do it best can intuit what their teammates are going to do because they know them that well.

When you know God at that level, fruit will be produced. You won't have to force it or fake it; you'll just create it. Or, rather, it will be created in you.

When Paul talks to us about the full knowledge of God, he's talking about entering into an experiential connection with God. He's talking about knowing God so deeply, fully, continually, and intentionally that your every move aligns with His in an unplanned cadence of connection. That's what it means to know God. And when you know Him at that level, fruit will be produced. You won't have to force it or fake it; you'll just create it. Or, rather, it will be created in you.

It is in God that you're supplied with all the wisdom you need to walk in the work He has for you to do (Colossians 1:9-10)—to bear fruit. God longs to produce something in you that is beautiful, enjoyable, and edible—fruit of impact, influence, and usefulness. God desires that your experience of knowing Him will give birth to luscious fruit in your character, conduct, and contributions. But, friend, that only comes about through intimacy with God Himself—through truly knowing Him.

No wife can get pregnant by having a discussion at the breakfast table with her husband about sex. Yes, she can talk about it with her husband every single day, and he can even say some pretty powerful things. In fact, both of them can talk about it for years. The length of time they talk makes no difference at all, because no wife is ever going to get pregnant from a discussion about the subject or knowledge of sex. She just isn't. There has to be a connected level of intimacy, an experiential knowing *(yada, epignosis)*, in order to instigate new life.

This is what Paul urges us toward in knowing God. Our experience with God is to be so rich, deep, and thick that we cannot help but bear fruit. And the only way that's done is through a process we call *abiding*. We learn about this process of abiding in John 15:1-4, where it says,

> I am the true vine, and My Father is the vinedresser. Every branch
> in Me that does not bear fruit, He takes away; and every branch
> that bears fruit, He prunes it so that it may bear more fruit. You are
> already clean because of the word which I have spoken to you. Abide
> in Me, and I in you. As the branch cannot bear fruit of itself unless
> it abides in the vine, so neither can you unless you abide in Me.

Here's the picture He paints for us: There's a great vineyard, a vine, a gardener, and branches that either bear fruit or do not. God is the gardener; Christ is the vine. You are a branch. Every branch that abides in Christ bears fruit. In fact, he or she bears *much* fruit. Conversely, no branch can bear fruit in and of itself. If and when there lacks an abiding presence in the vine, there also lacks fruit. Spiritual truths rarely come more simply put than this one.

Hang out with (abide in) Christ, and you will bear fruit.

Live apart from Christ, and you will not bear fruit.

Your bearing of fruit is entirely dependent on your relational intimacy with Jesus Christ. You can't skip that reality. You can't force fruit to grow. You can't even study it into existence. Fruit bearing all comes down to one very critical, yet also very simple, thing: abiding in Jesus Christ.

Abiding in Christ

This principle of abiding is so important that this one word shows up ten times in only six verses in John 15:

> *Abide* in Me … (verse 4)
>
> Unless it *abides* in the vine … (verse 4)
>
> Unless you *abide* in Me … (verse 4)
>
> He who *abides* in Me … (verse 5)
>
> If anyone does not *abide* in Me … (verse 6)
>
> If you *abide* in Me … (verse 7)
>
> My words *abide* in you … (verse 7)
>
> *Abide* in My love … (verse 9)
>
> You will *abide* in My love … (verse 10)
>
> And *abide* in His love … (verse 10)

Evidently, Jesus really wants us to know about this thing called abiding! What's more is that when Jesus was doing this critical teaching, He was personally addressing His male disciples. The entire context of the call to abide was a man speaking to men. I point this out because far too often, the call to draw close to Christ or have intimacy with God is seen as a feminine pursuit. But this principle of abiding is not solely a feminine calling. It applies to men as much as it does to women.

Jesus told men that without Him, they could not accomplish the great things He was preparing them to do (John 15:5). Yes, men, your greatness is tied to your abiding. And spiritual intimacy with our single Lord and Savior is critical to experiencing your real manhood as a single man. If you desire to live your life with momentum, strength, and success, you will need to implement this fundamental principle on a regular basis.

So what does it look like to abide in Christ? Well, we can start to understand this by discovering what it looks like to abide somewhere else. A number of years ago, my wife and I took a trip to the great, grape-growing countryside in Napa Valley, California. People come from all over America, and even from all around the world, to taste wine and see the miles and miles of vines blanketing the hills in scents of sweetness.

In a vineyard, you will always see the branches hoisted up and tied to a post. This is done so the grapes don't drag on the ground. If the grapes do drag on the ground, they'll never grow. They will become stuck in the dirt, unable to absorb any sunlight or receive a steady flow of nutrients. So the gardeners gently lift the grapes off the ground so they can grow to their potential.

You can't hang out in the dirt and get the sunshine; those two things are mutually exclusive.

One reason so many singles fail to produce fruit during this season of their lives is that they spend too much of their time settling in and around too much dirt. See, many singles are saying, "God, make me fruitful," but He won't do it because they don't want to be taken away from the "dirt" of sin. You must address unaddressed sin in your life if God is going to be free to lift you up and out of the dirt. You can't hang out in the dirt and get the sunshine; those two things are mutually exclusive.

Yet regardless of that reality, the dirt beckons more singles from the full expression of themselves than you may realize. Whether it's to numb feelings of loneliness, rejection, inadequacy, or fears of the future, there seems to be a tendency toward pursuits that provide a distraction rather than an investment in activities that produce development. Another fruit-related word for these distractions is *sucker shoots*.

Not all hindrances to producing fruit in a person's life occur in the dirt, either. Some hindrances happen from things that are seemingly good and beneficial in and of themselves. That's why the illustration given to us in John 15 goes into greater detail. We read, "Every branch in Me that does not bear fruit, He takes away; and every branch that bears fruit, He prunes it so that it may bear more fruit" (verse 2). Pruning is cutting away that which siphons off life.

Sucker shoots are little branches that show up on the vine and take away some of the nutrients designed to help the fruit to expand to its fullest potential. A sucker shoot is a diversion, simply put. It doesn't produce anything in and of itself. It just hangs out near the nutrients with no intention of developing anything from the nutrients it consumes. A sucker shoot takes from you what belongs to you, thus limiting in you what you need for you. It siphons off from you what is there to keep you flowing Godward.

In our personal lives, anyone or anything can be a sucker shoot. It can be a person, but it can also be television. It can even be a hobby. And while there may be nothing wrong with that person, TV show, or hobby, when it starts to rob you of what you need to develop your spiritual intimacy with Jesus, it has transitioned into a sucker shoot.

That's why the concept of moderation is so important. You have to create boundaries in your life to allow yourself the opportunity to abide. Abiding requires time. It requires repeat exposure. Compare abiding to the two types of tea drinkers. Some people like to dip their tea bag up and down in the hot water because they don't want their tea to get too strong. Others drop the tea bag in and just leave it there. That way the hot water can fully absorb all that the tea bag has to offer. When a tea bag abides in hot water, the tea becomes strong.

When you abide in Jesus Christ, your spiritual power, insight, and development become strong. You grow. Just like a baby in a mother's womb who gets his or her nutrients through the umbilical cord, the abiding connection produces growth. If there were to be a breach in the umbilical cord, there would also be a shrinking of life itself. It's the ongoing connection with the mother that keeps the baby growing and developing.

If you have ever fallen in love, you need no further illustration of what it means to abide. A text message here, a phone call there, time spent together—this is abiding. When people date, they don't just connect once a week for a few hours and call it done. In fact, when two people are deeply in love, they will abide in each other's presence on the phone way past the point where there's anything meaningful to say. They simply don't want to hang up. And then as soon as they do, one of them will text how much he or she is missing the other right now!

We know that's true in human relationships, yet we often fail to transfer that reality to our relationship with Jesus Christ. Far too many believers assume that a two-hour visit on Sunday morning is enough. Or perhaps they add on a Wednesday night, a verse in the morning, or a quick prayer when trouble pops up. But try applying the way you relate to Jesus to how you relate to other people in your life and see what happens. You might just lose a few friends and family members.

Try making every single conversation you have with a romantic partner, family member, or even a friend always about you and what you want them to do for you, and you might find yourself alone very quickly. But that's what most people do with Christ. They toss up a quick prayer of a wish list of sorts, and then they wonder why they're living such a fruitless, powerless, empty life. Jesus made it plain that without an intimate connection with Him, producing fruitfulness is impossible (John 15:5).

Jesus wants a relationship with you, not your religious activity. Sometimes it will be a five-second prayer just to let Him know you're thinking about Him. Other times it could be a five-minute prayer. Sometimes it will be deep. Other times it will be light. But the essence of abiding is that you are threading Jesus Christ (His presence, desires, and thoughts) through all that you think, do, and say. As 1 Corinthians 10:31 says, "Whether, then, you eat or drink or whatever you do, do all to the glory of God."

What too many people want is a microwave experience of God when He's offering a Crockpot experience. They want to go to church and push a button for some quick results. But you know the truth about microwaved food just as well as I do. It can get real hot really quickly, but it can also then get real cold really quickly. That's because the food did not abide in the presence of that which heats it, leaving it briefly hot on the outside but cold on the inside.

It's in the abiding that you'll discover the fruit. And it's only in the abiding. Which is why singleness offers most people a greater opportunity for spiritual growth, development, and productivity than they realize is possible.

> *Look for the gaps that singleness gives you as gifts to cultivate your abiding relationship with Jesus Christ.*

I'm not saying that schedules are less full for singles than they are for married folks. Many singles today have kids to raise and often juggle a couple of jobs just to pay the bills. I understand the complexities and the time demands of singleness. I've seen it firsthand with two of my children over the years, as well as with other family members and the myriad of singles in our church. But what singles do have is that gap in those times that allow them mentally and emotionally to focus Godward. They are gaps that so often are eaten up by the demands, duties, and even delights of marriage. But they still do exist for singles.

Yes, as you read this you may feel busy and overwhelmed, and your schedule might support those feelings. But look for the gaps that singleness gives you as gifts to cultivate your abiding relationship with Jesus Christ. Seize those moments, and guard them fiercely. He's worth it. You're worth it. And the fruit produced both in you and through you to affect others for good is worth it. Oftentimes singleness is the most productive season in a person's life toward goals, desires, and even dreams. Don't waste it in a perpetual state of busy, seeking to fill the gaps with sucker shoots or distractions. Rather, embrace the gaps life has to offer, and discover a depth of knowing God such as you never even imagined possible.

He longs for you to know Him that way. He longs for your company, your voice, your presence, and your conversations. The fruit will come, but it will come as a byproduct of tapping into and staying connected with Jesus Christ, which in turn will enable your character to reflect His in every way, shape, and form.

9

SINGLE BUT NOT ALONE

As a citizen of the United States or another nation, you have certain rights and privileges that come with your citizenship. Because you belong to that country, there are legal rights to which you can appeal. It's your homeland, your community.

If you're a believer, you belong to another nation as well. You're a citizen of the kingdom of God. Your birthright as a citizen of God's kingdom affords you various rights and privileges. Of course, if you don't know those rights or don't access those rights, you're not living as a full beneficiary of those rights. But that does not negate the reality that you have them.

In the same vein, in America, some of our rights are assigned to us as individuals (e.g., the rights to life, liberty, and the pursuit of happiness), whereas other rights are carried out as a group (e.g., the rights to protection from warring nations and to choose our elected officials). Similarly, some of the rights you have as a believer are yours to live out individually, but other privileges come to you in a group setting. Jesus introduces us to two of these group rights in Matthew 18, where we read,

If your brother sins, go and show him his fault in private; if he
listens to you, you have won your brother. But if he does not
listen to you, take one or two more with you, so that by the
mouth of two or three witnesses every fact may be confirmed.
If he refuses to listen to them, tell it to the church; and if he refuses
to listen even to the church, let him be to you as a Gentile and a
tax collector. Truly I say to you, whatever you bind on earth shall
have been bound in heaven; and whatever you loose on earth shall
have been loosed in heaven. Again I say to you, that if two of you
agree on earth about anything that they may ask, it shall be done
for them by My Father who is in heaven. For where two or three
have gathered together in My name, I am there in their midst.
(Matthew 18:15-20)

Unfortunately, far too many people today limit their definition of the
church to the place where they go on Sunday for spiritual information and
inspiration. And while the church is that place to come to for a sermon and
music, you don't really need the church for that. You could listen to a sermon on a CD or digital download, or you could stream your music. But
Jesus made the church His key agency in history because there is far more
to the entity of the church than just preaching and singing. The church is
that legislative body (ecclesia) whereby we are endowed with certain collective rights in community that enable us to have institutional and legal access to call down heaven into affairs on Earth beyond that which we could
do individually.

Bringing Heaven to Earth

Many churches have limited themselves merely to inspiration and educa-
tion, skipping legislation altogether, but Jesus makes it clear that this is the
method to effectively carrying out our rule and influence as His body on

Earth. In Matthew 18:18 we read (as Jesus addressed the subject of the church), "Truly I say to you, whatever you bind on earth shall have been bound in heaven; and whatever you loose on earth shall have been loosed in heaven."

Please notice something: It is God's people who do the binding and the loosing. It's not God binding and loosing; it's you doing it, with God backing it up. Thus, if you don't know what to bind or what to loose, you won't have heaven helping you out in history. What's more, if you don't know how to connect in community with other believers who can also tap into this legal authority, you will simply be speaking words into thin air. Only the church possesses the keys to the kingdom, giving it corporate authority to bind and loose in history (Matthew 16:18-19).

I realize that for singles, finding a sense of community in the church can be a challenge. It seems that a lot of the social events, small groups, and other activities are geared toward families. And perhaps many of the singles' events are focused more on activities centered on "talking about singleness" rather than truly connecting people in meaningful ways. So as a single Christian living in the context of a culture that doesn't naturally promote community, you need to be more intentional about finding meaningful community in a church setting. Because it's not just for the purpose of socializing; it's for the purpose of exercising authority on Earth.

If you're being held hostage today by difficulties, challenges, or sins that you have sought to overcome on your own, it may be because you've sought to address them on your own. Jesus emphasizes this truth in Matthew 18:19-20, which we read earlier: "Again I say to you, that if two of you agree on earth about anything that they may ask, it shall be done for them by My Father who is in heaven. For where two or three have gathered together in My name, I am there in their midst."

The phrase "two or three" is an Old Testament phrase. Jesus didn't just make it up. In Deuteronomy 19:15 we read, "A single witness shall not rise up against a man on account of any iniquity or any sin which he has committed; on the evidence of two or three witnesses a matter shall be confirmed." Deuteronomy 17:6 says, "On the evidence of two witnesses or three witnesses, he who is to die shall be put to death; he shall not be put to death on the evidence of one witness." Thus, when Jesus references "two or three," He is reaching back into the Old Testament legal culture to explain to the church the power of the New Testament age. He is saying that two or three witnesses were designated to make something official and legal in the spiritual realm.

The term *agree* used in Matthew 18:19 comes from the Greek word *symphoneo*, which literally means "symphony." That term also means "in alignment" or "to be on the same page." And this is why the context of church community is so critical. Through the fellowship under the collective umbrella of the church, you are able to unleash heaven's authority and power in a far greater manner than you could ever do on your own.

God has created community within the church to act as the legitimate authority to legislate from heaven. Your active engagement and connection with community in the church provides you with the opportunity for relationships with others who are spiritually in sync with you so that together, you're more effective at ruling on Earth. As I said, it's not enough to simply come to church to hear a sermon. In fact, I hate to bring this up, but oftentimes I'll run into church members mid-week and ask about last Sunday's sermon. All I get in response is some stumbling around with their words and a sheepish look on their faces. They don't even remember it!

∽०∾

Church is to be the context for community.

∽०∾

Church is to be the context for community, not just the context for spiritual inspiration and information. And through the power of community, you are to discover and unleash the power that's rightfully yours. In Exodus 17, we read the popular story of a battle between Israel and an enemy. While Joshua and Israel's army fought relentlessly in the valley,

Moses stood on the mountaintop and held up the rod of God.

As we discover in the passage relaying the details of this battle, the victory Joshua and the army experienced in the valley was directly tied to their connection with Moses and his actions on the summit. It says,

> So it came about when Moses held his hand up, that Israel prevailed, and when he let his hand down, Amalek prevailed. But Moses' hands were heavy. Then they took a stone and put it under him, and he sat on it; and Aaron and Hur supported his hands, one on one side and one on the other. Thus his hands were steady until the sun set. So Joshua overwhelmed Amalek and his people with the edge of the sword. (Exodus 17:11–13)

In other words, what Moses did up top determined the success or failure down below. I'm sure that a number of people reading this book know what it's like to be doing the very best you can, trying the hardest that you're able, but failing time and time again. This is because we have neglected this all-important emphasis on community in the church. Not only that, but this issue seems to take its toll more so on singles than on anyone else, simply because singles are often more isolated.

That's why I can't stress enough the importance of linking up as a single with other like-minded believers (whether they're also single is irrelevant) and maintaining an atmosphere of community. Far too often, I see more and more singles attend church less and less. For whatever reason, there tends to be a pattern where singles come and go as they please. And while that negatively affects their own spiritual development, it also severely limits their ability to overcome, move forward, and legislate heaven's rule on Earth—in their own lives and in the spheres of influence in which God has placed them.

Friend, you may think you can make it as a lone-ranger Christian, but I want to serve notice that if you don't consistently have spiritually minded people who are tight with God in your life—either to hold your own arms up when you get tired or to hold up the rod when you battle in the valley—you will never experience all that God has for you to experience. That's why the goal of the church ought to be to bring people along through discipleship in order to increase their spiritual maturity and align them with others.

Keep in mind, there is a condition to Christ's commission of joint power in prayer. We saw it in Matthew 18:20: "For where two or three have gathered together in My name, I am there in their midst." It's His name.

Community in and of itself does not unleash the power to bind, loose, and gain victory in your life. Rather, it's community centered on Christ's name, where He is in the midst. Jesus Christ must be in the middle of it. Scripture tells us plainly that there is one, and only one, mediator between heaven and Earth, which is the Lord Jesus Christ (1 Timothy 2:5). Jesus is called the Son of God, and He's also called the Son of Man. He is called both because He has two natures in one personhood, unmixed forever. We refer to this as the hypostatic union. Because of this unique position, Jesus is able to reach into heaven yet also grab Earth at the same time. His role is to listen to us on Earth while connecting us with the Father above. That's why we're told He "intercedes" for us (Romans 8:34).

For Jesus to be "in the midst," and for us to gain the full manifestation of His power, we must be connected in community. As a single, without the natural community of a spouse to lean on, you must intentionally seek out regular, ongoing, spiritual community. With it, you'll access the authentic power of Christ's name at the highest level available.

Not too long ago, a staff member told me that there were thirteen fake Tony Evans Twitter accounts online. Thirteen! These folks were using my name in order to swindle people out of money. That's called forgery. Forgery is the unauthorized use of another person's name for the benefit of yourself.

So we contacted Twitter and had those thirteen accounts shut down!

Now, as you might imagine, new accounts popped up just as quickly as we shut those others down. But my point is that many Christians are praying in Jesus' name, or using Jesus' name, without the authentic connection with others and with Him in Jesus' name. And thus what they're asking for is not being accessed. You can pray in Jesus' name all day long, but if you're not rightfully aligned under God's kingdom agenda and within His will, as well as in sync with those around you when you ask, Jesus does not guarantee the answer you desire. Only when your will surrenders to God's will and you join forces with others who are like-minded does He guarantee you will receive that for which you ask. Jesus desires to have a relational presence in your life and in your social network. He desires to be smack-dab in the middle of who you are and those you hang with. This is because when He's in the midst, miracles happen.

Your church body should be a spiritual family wherein you can experience community as part of a larger group under God. Remember, it is "Our Father who art in heaven," not "My Daddy who is in heaven." While every single is an individual, it must be clearly understood that God rejects individualism. It's in the context of accountability within the community of believers that you're to find a balance between keeping your personal uniqueness and avoiding illegitimate codependence on unhealthy relationships.

> *While every single is an individual, it must be clearly understood that God rejects individualism.*

You've been made a part of something that's bigger and is meant to be more than a place where you come sit and hear a sermon or be sung to. It's a place where you're responsible and accountable in community. If that's not happening in your life, and if Sunday morning is simply a spectator sport where you take in a performance, then you're not positioning yourself to fully maximize your life as a kingdom single—or to be fully delivered from that which holds you down.

Help in Community

If you're only a Sunday spectator, you're also not positioning yourself for help in those times you may need it most. We have countless stories of singles who received help in the context of the church community where I pastor. I remember one in particular because of how drastic her needs were. She had become a widow suddenly. Yet because she was part of the church, the church rallied around her to provide her needs. These were practical needs during this initial time of grief, such as doing her shopping for her, taking her kids to school, running errands, and things of that nature. Once she was able to do these things for herself, she did. But in her time of great need, the church was there for her.

Another woman moved to Dallas as a single parent and began attending our church. She was a high school dropout but middle-aged by then. The church became her support system, providing her tutoring and the pathway to get her GED. Folks arranged free childcare for her kids in the times she needed to go to school. The church also set her up with a mentor to help her make life choices that would get her on her feet. Lastly, after she got her GED, our church helped her get a good job.

These are just two examples of hundreds upon hundreds. As a single, you too may come upon times when you have practical needs, and being part of a local body of believers will give you the opportunity to have others help you when you do.

In Mark 2, we read about the power that comes from community. We're introduced to a man who is helpless due to paralysis. Yet since this man is not alone, and since his community of friends is in the midst of Jesus, this man's entire life gets set upright. It says,

When He [Jesus] had come back to Capernaum several days
afterward, it was heard that He was at home. And many were
gathered together, so that there was no longer room, not even near
the door; and He was speaking the word to them. And they came,
bringing to Him a paralytic, carried by four men. Being unable
to get to Him because of the crowd, they removed the roof above
Him; and when they had dug an opening, they let down the pallet
on which the paralytic was lying. (Mark 2:1-4)

There are times in life when the only way up, over, or through is with
the help of others. This story illustrates that principle fully. It may not be a
physical paralysis you're facing, but you could be stuck and unable to move
from where you are. Some paralysis is emotional, when you simply can't
shake how you feel. You can't shake the mental anguish of what you've
gone through.

Maybe a situation happened years ago, but it still dominates your mind
and your thinking. You can't forget it, move past it, get over it, or be loosed
from it. It's a mental paralysis that stops you from getting to where you
need to go.

There's also circumstantial paralysis that could be holding you hostage,
whether it's codependency with another person or a circumstance where
you feel stuck in a career without a calling. It may be a particular boss,
coworker, or position that keeps you down. Or it could be a financial paralysis that just becomes deeper and deeper with each passing day. It feels
like a never-ending cycle of perpetual debt. Whatever it is, there's one thing
consistent about paralysis: You can't get out of it on your own.

Thus, similar to the way the man in the story was maneuvered and
lifted by his community of friends, we often need help to get out of a situation that we cannot break free of on our own. That's why community is so
critical.

At times, it's your close friends who can either help you along or you can help them along. But then other times the church community may provide growth opportunities not specifically tied to friendships. Because of the proximity of like-minded believers, you're lifted up.

A situation like this is found in Acts 3:1-10, where Peter and John were heading to the temple to worship. On their way, they came across a beggar who had been lame from birth, sitting outside the gate called Beautiful. Rather than toss some coins into the beggar's coffer for a temporary fix, Peter and John urged him to look at them instead. And just as Jesus was in the midst of the situation with the paralytic who received his healing, Peter and John invited Jesus into the midst of what they did next. We read,

> But Peter said, "I do not possess silver and gold, but what I do have I give to you: In the name of Jesus Christ the Nazarene—walk!" And seizing him by the right hand, he raised him up; and immediately his feet and his ankles were strengthened. With a leap he stood upright and began to walk; and he entered the temple with them, walking and leaping and praising God. (Acts 3:6-9)

This lame man had to go to the temple gate every single day, simply for sustenance to get by. He was eking out a living through begging. But because he chose to position himself in the context of the church community, he ran across two men who were able to give him much more than a few coins. They gave him the ability to stand on his own, work on his own, and gain the dignity and strength he needed to fully live his life.

Community isn't always defined by your friendships, although friends are critical and important. Placing yourself among like-minded believers who know how to call on the name of Jesus and invite Him into the midst of a situation is community as well. I understand that singleness lends itself to certain difficulties and challenges, and that finding an ongoing atmosphere of community is often one of them. When there's no one in your home to whom you may be accountable, it's far easier to offer up an excuse and skip church, Bible study, small group, or serving opportunities. However, when you do, you're setting yourself up for a life that lacks the full power you need to overcome the challenges you face. You are also limiting your own ability to help and empower others in Jesus' name.

Remember my key illustration from chapter 1—how the key ring held two distinct and unique keys that did not lose their uniqueness but were brought into proximity by the ring? Each key on a key ring is whole all by itself. And if you're like me, you have a number of keys on your key ring, all of them complete.

Community provides the context for you to be maximized by God to your greatest potential.

Yet because they're surrounded by other keys and all together, they are now in a community of keys that enable me to access each one a lot more freely and fully than I could if they were spread all over the house or all over my office somewhere. Likewise, community provides the context for you to be maximized by God to your greatest potential.

Other Benefits of Community

In addition to the benefits of community we've looked at so far, there are others as well. For example, the context of community enables you to better discover your own gifts and talents (1 Corinthians 12:1-11). It allows you the opportunity to identify needs that other people may have that God wants you to help meet (1 Thessalonians 5:14). Community positions you for spiritual growth, maturity, and even physical healing (James 5:16). It provides a place to both offer encouragement and receive it (Hebrews 10:24-25). And it lightens the load you may be carrying on your own as a single (Galatians 6:2).

Most of all, community gives you a place where you truly belong

(Romans 12:5), and in today's increasingly isolated culture, this is far more important than many of us may admit or even realize. If you're a selfish single, concerned only with being blessed and not being a blessing to others in the context of the local church, you'll limit what God will do for you because you won't allow Him to work through you for the benefit of others.

One of the movies we all grew up watching was *The Wizard of Oz*. The girl's name is Dorothy, and she's from Kansas. Through a tornado and its effect, Dorothy is whisked away to a whole new world of munchkins, monkeys, witches, and poppies. Now, Dorothy and her dog, Toto, want to go home to Kansas, but they can't. Instead, they are stuck in the middle of a battle between the good witch and the bad witch, and they're told to head to an Emerald City to seek the blessing of the great, powerful Oz. This great, powerful Oz supposedly holds the power to get Dorothy and Toto back to where they want to go.

Instructed to follow the yellow brick road, Dorothy sets out on a journey. Along the way, she discovers a community who will go on this journey with her. She finds a scarecrow without a brain, a lion without much courage, and a tin man without a heart. Soon Dorothy's trip of two has become a trip of five, as they all set out with different needs to satisfy.

Now, let's be clear. On their way to Oz, they run into some problems. Evil strategies seek to block them, crazy flying monkeys try to disturb them, poppies lure them to sleep, and all sorts of chaos seeks to disconnect them from each other. Yet somehow, they stay closely connected as a community, walking, singing, dancing, and pushing forward together until they finally make it to Oz.

Once they reach Oz, they discover that the power they were looking for in a wizard (who turns out to be human) was really within them from the start. All Dorothy needed to do was click her heels three times and she would be back home. All the scarecrow needed to do was believe in himself. The tin man needed to open up his emotions. And the lion needed to know he was stronger than he thought. But none of them would have discovered the powers they had access to if they hadn't traveled together in search of what they needed.

Friend, may I encourage you, as you head down your own yellow brick road, that the pathway laid out for you based on God's Word will lead you exactly where you need to go as a kingdom single. God is not finished with you, or with those He places in your circle. Even though your needs may be different from those of the people with whom you link arms, God will meet each of your needs in His own unique way by revealing His power within through the presence of Jesus Christ. Never neglect connecting with others through your journey of singleness. Together, you will discover that home has always been much closer than you think.

PART III

THE CONCERNS OF A KINGDOM SINGLE

10

SEEKING A MATE

Not everyone who is single is looking for a spouse. Many people are fully maximizing their singleness and are content with their status. But then there are those of you reading who are absolutely certain you want to get married. You know the Bible says that whoever finds a wife finds a good thing and finds favor from the Lord (Proverbs 18:22), and you wish to experience that favor or to be the vessel of favor that someone else finds. You desire to be married, feel led to get married, dream of being married, but have not yet come upon the path to getting married. You don't want to go to the club. You're tired of scrolling through pictures of people online. You believe the Lord has a future spouse out there for you; you just don't know how to locate him or her.

If that's you, this chapter is written for you.

In Genesis 24, we find four primary concerns for the single who wants to be married. I want to introduce these by starting in verses 31-33, which say,

And he said, "Come in, blessed of the LORD! Why do you stand outside since I have prepared the house, and a place for the camels?" So the man entered the house. Then Laban unloaded the camels, and he gave straw and feed to the camels, and water to wash his feet

and the feet of the men who were with him. But when food was
set before him to eat, he said, "I will not eat until I have told my
business."

What is the business the man wanted to tell? It was the business concerning a marriage. The context of this story involves Abraham, who was
now aged and had a son who was forty years old and still single. His son's
name was Isaac. Abraham wanted his son to get married, as is the case with
most parents. But his son, for whatever reason, had not found the right
person. And with Isaac at forty years old, with the clock of Abraham's
promise of heirs ticking in his single son, Abraham grew increasingly concerned about finding a wife for Isaac. That's the scenario for the passage we
just read.

What the entirety of chapter 24 in Genesis does is unfold this divine
process of connecting Isaac with his future wife Rebekah. Within this process are the concerns we're going to look at if you're in need of a miracle for
a relationship and marriage in your own life.

Total Commitment to God

The first concern is found in the principle of total commitment to God. We
see this in Genesis 24:2-4:

Abraham said to his servant, the oldest of his household, who
had charge of all that he owned, "Please place your hand under my
thigh, and I will make you swear by the LORD, the God of heaven
and the God of earth, that you shall not take a wife for my son from
the daughters of the Canaanites, among whom I live, but you will
go to my country and to my relatives, and take a wife for my son
Isaac."

It's important to note that Abraham and his male servant were two men who were spiritually concerned for the kind of woman Isaac was marrying. Why? Because the issue was bigger than just finding a wife. It involved preserving and continuing a divine covenant.

Single men, you must open your eyes and see the importance of choosing your wife from a spiritual standpoint. One of the reasons this isn't occurring as much as it should is that we lack in the Body of Christ men like Abraham and his servant—kingdom men who will help the single men understand and make spiritual choices of a mate. The woman you marry will help solidify your legacy as a man, for good or for bad. She will heavily influence your children and children's children, for good or for bad. Hormones and external shape and beauty alone should not have more say than heaven in what kind of woman you seek.

> *Single men, you must open your eyes and see the importance of choosing your wife from a spiritual standpoint.*

Abraham told his servant, in the name of the Lord, that finding the right wife for his son needed divine intervention. She also needed to come from those who were rightly aligned under God's kingdom program. Abraham understood that this was a very serious decision that would lead to a very serious commitment. Which is why he made his servant pledge an oath to God that he would not look for a wife outside of those within the family of God at that time, his own relatives. *God had to be brought into the process of the natural for the supernatural to occur.*

We discover that the reason Abraham wanted this was a covenant. God had made a covenant with Abraham, and that covenant involved the kingdom blessing to all people through his seed. Thus, he wanted the servant to get a wife for his son to fulfill the covenant of God, which meant he could not take a wife from the nearby pagan Canaanites. Abraham was making a commitment not to compromise on the wife for his son. Even though his son was getting older, Abraham did not seek a quick solution. He sought a God-ordained solution so that he could honor the covenant God had made with him. Rebekah's commitment was also demonstrated by the fact that she maintained her moral purity (Genesis 24:16).

If you want God in the process of finding your future mate, there must be a radical commitment to Him up front. Yes, it would have been easy to go to the nearby Canaanites to find a wife for Isaac, but that would have excluded God from the process.

When you're seeking a mate, be sure you're willing to commit to the principles of God's kingdom over and above simply trying to fill a slot on your dance card. Second Corinthians 6:14-16 says,

> Do not be bound together with unbelievers; for what partnership have righteousness and lawlessness, or what fellowship has light with darkness? Or what harmony has Christ with Belial, or what has a believer in common with an unbeliever? Or what agreement has the temple of God with idols? For we are the temple of the living God.

It's like the man who met a beautiful woman at the airport and asked where she was going. She told him she was flying to Florida. He told her he was flying to Canada. Then he asked if they could fly together. Of course, you realize that's not possible—just as it's not possible to have a kingdom marriage if one of the two spouses is not aligned under God's kingdom rule or seeking His will in his or her life. Abraham didn't ask his servant to get a wife from the Canaanites for his son and then lead the wife to God. No, he made a clear commitment up front that the future wife they were seeking for the family would already know and serve the Lord.

Confidence in God

The second concern we learn from Genesis 24 is to not only have commitment to God, but to also be concerned with your level of confidence in Him. In verse 7 we read, "The LORD, the God of heaven, who took me from my father's house and from the land of my birth, and who spoke to me and who swore to me, saying, 'To your descendants I will give this land,' He will send His angel before you, and you will take a wife for my son from there."

In this verse, we see Abraham demonstrating faith in divine guidance. He was exercising a conviction that when he was fully committed to God in this pursuit, God would lead his servant to the right person.

Thus, based on that commitment and conviction, the servant took the ten camels from his master and set out to find a wife for Isaac. In other words, he also stepped out in faith. He wasn't passive. His actions indicated that he too believed that if he honored God, God would lead him to the right person for Isaac to marry. Scripture says, "He who finds a wife finds a good thing and obtains favor from the LORD" (Proverbs 18:22). Therefore, it's okay to search for a person God has for you, as well as to make yourself locatable, as long as you search spiritually and not carnally.

Specific Prayers

The third concern we discover in this story arose when the servant reached the land to which he was sent. After arriving, he settled down and prayed to God. We read,

> He said, "O LORD, the God of my master Abraham, please grant me success today, and show lovingkindness to my master Abraham. Behold, I am standing by the spring, and the daughters of the men of

the city are coming out to draw water; now may it be that the girl to whom I say, 'Please let down your jar so that I may drink,' and who answers, 'Drink, and I will water your camels also'—may she be the one whom You have appointed for Your servant Isaac; and by this I will know that You have shown lovingkindness to my master."
(Genesis 24:12-14)

This concern involves becoming specific in your prayers and expectations about what you're hoping for in a mate, as well as asking God to grant you success in finding one. The servant's faith was so deep that he made a specific request to God at a specific time about a specific situation, asking God to address it in a specific way. He didn't just pray, "Lord, bless me and bring me a wife for Isaac." No, he asked God to bless him that very day, to arrange his steps at a certain well to bring the right person across his path in a certain way.

Friend, let me ask you a question. When was the last time you wrote down what you wanted in a future mate and showed it to God? When was the last time you prayed to God with specific traits, character qualities, and even circumstances to tell God this is exactly what you're looking for? Or do you just say, "God, I'm tired of being alone. Please bring me someone, anyone." Because if that vague request is what you pray, that's what you'll get. The attitude of prayer is a specific attitude, and God responds to our requests at the level that we give them.

> *When was the last time you wrote down what you wanted in a future mate and showed it to God?*

Consider what would happen if you told Amazon's Alexa to order you some soap. You probably wouldn't get anything at all, because Alexa would need to know what kind of soap you wanted, how much you wanted, and how soon you wanted it. If you were unwilling to engage Alexa in a conversation of that depth, your order for soap would simply never be created. And yet while we understand how to be specific when we're ordering things to buy, we often fail to be specific in our communication with God and then wonder why our prayers never seem to get answered.

If you haven't done so already and you desire a mate, would you write down the characteristics you're looking for in a prayer to God? And then revisit it regularly as you continue to pray, and even fast, over those qualities, adding to them or taking away as you feel you need to. I've known many singles who carried this principle out in prayer and then found their future spouse not long afterward.

The qualities and test that the servant requested of God for the future wife of Isaac were not random. Asking her to draw water for his camels revealed a number of Rebekah's character traits, such as kindness, work ethic, generosity, and more. It meant that of all the women there, she was the one who was industrious. Remember, Abraham's servant had ten camels. A thirsty camel can drink twenty-five gallons of water. That's a lot of water for a woman to draw. So in asking God for the answer to his prayer to come in the form that it did, he was looking for a woman who was productive, giving, and strong.

Not only that, but he was also looking for a woman of integrity. He found just that: "The girl was very beautiful, a virgin, and no man had had relations with her; and she went down to the spring and filled her jar and came up" (Genesis 24:16).

Integrity is a critical concern in seeking a mate. The level of integrity in your future spouse will figure heavily into the quality and effectiveness of your future marriage for the kingdom. Integrity is more than reputation. Reputation is what other people think about you. Integrity ties into character and has to do with who you are when no one else is observing. In order to possess integrity, there must be a moral code that governs your decisions.

The word *integrity* means to be undivided. It stems from being true to one's ethical standards and without compromise. Proverbs 20:6-7 tells us that finding people of integrity is hard to do. Those who possess it will often stand apart from the crowd.

The Integrity of a Daniel

So important is this area of integrity that I want to look at it a bit further in the life of Daniel, a godly man never identified as having been married. Daniel's story occurred in a culture where his people, the Israelites, had been taken captive by the Babylonians. They were now living in a pagan, secular environment that was full of idolatry and run by a king who thought he was a god, Nebuchadnezzar.

It is critical that single Christian men emulate Daniel's example, not yielding to the culture, but rather maintaining their biblical standard before the culture.

The reason I point out the context of the culture is to emphasize that integrity has nothing to do with a person's surroundings. It has everything to do with the person. Similar to Joseph in Egypt, Daniel lived a life of character in the midst of cultural chaos, much like our world today.

Yet, even as a teenager, Daniel showed his integrity as a kingdom single man when he refused to compromise with idolatry by eating the meat that had been sacrificed to idols (Daniel 1:8). He also surrounded himself with other kingdom single men who shared his values (i.e., Meshach, Shadrach, and Abed-nego) (Daniel 1:19-20; 2:17-18, 49).

It is critical that single Christian men emulate Daniel's example, not yielding to the culture, but rather maintaining their biblical standard before the culture. They should also surround themselves with other single brothers who are pursuing becoming kingdom men so they can battle together against the ungodly influence of the world. That's not to say that living with values and virtues won't cause any issues, men. But it is saying that God will be in the midst of those to fight the battles for you, just as He was with Daniel.

Because Daniel had distinguished himself with a solid work ethic and sound character, he was quickly promoted (Daniel 6:1-3). Now, of course, with promotion often comes jealousy. And those who worked alongside Daniel sought to bring him down. In verses 4-5 we read,

> Then the commissioners and satraps began trying to find a ground
> of accusation against Daniel in regard to government affairs; but
> they could find no ground of accusation or evidence of corruption,
> inasmuch as he was faithful, and no negligence or corruption was
> to be found in him. Then these men said, "We will not find any
> ground of accusation against this Daniel unless we find it against
> him with regard to the law of his God."

In their search to trap Daniel in wrongdoing, they could find nothing. So they sought to frame Daniel using his own convictions to God. Thus, they created a scheme in which they got the king to agree to a decree stating that no one could pray to any other god but him for a full thirty days. The consequence of such a crime would be the lions' den.

Despite risk to his very life, though, Daniel continued to pray to the one, true God every single day. In fact, he did so boldly—with his window open, so all could see. That's integrity. Many could have argued that Daniel needed to play politics in order to save his life and remain an influence in the Babylonian kingdom. But Daniel knew better. He knew that there was no playing when it came to God and where his spiritual loyalty was. Rather than take a sabbatical from religious duties, Daniel "continued kneeling on his knees three times a day, praying and giving thanks before his God, as he had been doing previously" (Daniel 6:10).

It's been said that integrity is only tested under pressure. Like a tea bag, you never know how strong it is until it's in hot water. As a result of Daniel's character, he was found guilty of breaking the king's decree. And even though the king loved Daniel (Daniel 6:14), he couldn't revoke the law. So Daniel wound up being tossed to the lions.

You probably know the outcome of this story. God shut the mouths of the lions, and Daniel remained unharmed throughout the night. In the morning, the king rushed to the den to see if Daniel was still there. And he was. See, God knows how to make your enemies your footstool when He needs to. He knows how to turn things, flip them, and tweak them to His advantage when you're committed to Him. That is why it's absolutely critical that one of your highest concerns in seeking a future mate be this person's level of integrity. Marriage (and life) is hard enough as it is. But when you add a lack of character into the equation, you will quickly find yourself off the path of divine favor and provision.

Abraham's servant had asked for a very specific woman to be the wife for Isaac. He sought a woman of character, integrity, and purity. As a result, God granted him his request.

God's Confirmation

This leads us to our fourth concern when looking for a future spouse, and that's the concern of confirmation. Friend, always carry a concern with you when you're dating or looking to marriage that God will confirm your situation and your relationship. Never proceed without His confirmation.

While everything may look as if it's adding up and you've found "the one," it is critical that you don't drop God from the equation when you fall in love. Marriage is such an important, lifelong decision that making sure this is a good person for you to marry cannot be emphasized enough. This is why asking God to confirm your relationship before you make it official is the fourth concern we're looking at from this biblical example.

God can confirm things for us in numbers of ways. Most often, His confirmation comes through Scripture. But another way He confirms things is through "two or three witnesses" (Deuteronomy 19:15; Matthew 18:16; 2 Corinthians 13:1)—when He gives other people the same belief as you that this is His will. Conversely, it's a certain red flag if your closest spiritual friends, pastor, and/or family are advising you that the person you're dating is not "marriage material." Never let your emotions override the loving advice of those around you. Know that if it's God's will, He has the power to change the hearts of those around you, giving them the same confidence in your relationship as you have.

We see in Genesis 24 that after the servant spent time with Rebekah and her family, Rebekah's family had the same conviction he did. In verses 50-51 we read, "Then Laban and Bethuel replied, 'The matter comes from the LORD; so we cannot speak to you bad or good. Here is Rebekah before you, take her and go, and let her be the wife of your master's son, as the LORD has spoken.'"

If God is leading you, He's going to tell someone else who is spiritually in tune with His kingdom purposes.

Friend, if God is leading you, He's going to tell someone else who is spiritually in tune with His kingdom purposes. Rebekah's family confirmed what the servant believed to be true. And further into the passage, we read that Rebekah confirmed it as well: "And they said, 'We will call the girl and consult her wishes.' Then they called Rebekah and said to her, 'Will you go with this man?' And she said, 'I will go'" (Genesis 24:57-58).

Keep in mind, Rebekah was going to somebody she'd never even met. But when you have a clear direction from God, the natural course of things doesn't matter so much. It doesn't have to take long. You don't have to jump through all the hoops or wait for the timing that seems "right." When God is in it, He will make it completely clear.

I know people who have dated for three years and are still asking if this is the one. If you don't know after three years, I can answer that question for you. And it's *no*. It doesn't have to take long when God is involved, and confirmation occurs both within and without. When God is moving, it becomes inexplicably clear. Isn't that what happened to Ruth in the Bible? Ruth committed herself to God by committing herself to Naomi. Soon afterward, God connected her with Boaz, who observed the quality of her character (Ruth 2:10-13).

When God is in the midst, He moves things around and does the miraculous.

He did it for Ruth and Boaz. He did it for Rebekah and Isaac. And in the biggest marriage arrangement ever, He did it for Joseph and Mary in order to fulfill His kingdom plan of giving the world the Messiah through both the legal and biological lineage of David. And He can do it for you, regardless of what the statistics say.

We read in the Genesis story that Rebekah rode home with the servant to marry a man she had never seen before, and when they met, they soon fell in love. People often ask me if I believe in love at first sight. My answer is *yes*. If God is in it, I believe people can fall in love quickly. Because when God is in it, He has already prepared both people long before they met.

If you are asking God for a spouse, remember these four primary concerns: Commit yourself to God, move forward with confidence in Him, tell God specifically what you're looking for in a mate regarding character and integrity, and ask Him for confirmation when you think you've found it. God can provide when you seek Him according to His will and rule as king over your life. The more committed you are to being a kingdom single, the better position you're in to discover a kingdom relationship.

11

⚋⚬⚋

SINGLES AND SEX,
PART 1

Bowlers take their sport very seriously. A friend of mine bowls in competition, and it's amazing to watch the enthusiasm that goes into each event. I don't know about you, but I'm what you would call a "casual" bowler. I enjoy a game of bowling occasionally, but that's it. I don't have a special outfit that I wear, special shoes, or even a special bowling ball. If my family feels like bowling, we'll head to the bowling alley, pay for our game, and use the things that are available to us there.

But when serious bowlers want to play a game, you can be sure they come with their own shoes, ball, gloves, towel, and everything else that may be needed.

That's the difference between serious bowlers and casual bowlers. Casual bowlers will use any ball that comes up the track, simply because that's what's available. Now, keep in mind, those balls are often chipped, cracked, or scuffed since so many people have used them. But serious bowlers have their own customized bowling balls. They're special to their owners, and serious bowlers hold them as sacred. In fact, they're the only ones who use these customized balls, because they've been built with the bowler in mind. Customized balls come at a high cost, but they also allow bowlers to engage in the experience at a higher, more meaningful level than they could otherwise.

Friend, you are custom-made by Christ and have been bought at a high price (1 Corinthians 6:20). Your sexuality is meant to be engaged with and experienced by one person only—your future spouse. You are not to allow yourself to be used up, chipped, scuffed, and devalued through casual sex. Otherwise, when it comes time for you to marry, you'll have nothing better to offer the love of your life than what is left. In fact, God uses sexual purity as a tangible test of your level of spiritual growth and maturity (1 Thessalonians 4:3-6).

To say that God puts a very high value on sexual purity is to understate it. The reason people give sex away so easily is that they don't know how valuable sexual purity is in God's eyes. Things that you think are cheap, you throw away. Things that you think are expensive and valuable, you hold onto. When God created Adam and Eve as opposite yet complementary sexual beings with a natural attraction for each other, Adam's statements about Eve in Genesis 2:23 show he understood that they were created for each other. And when God joined that first pair in marriage, there was no hesitation and no shame in their union. Theirs was the first and only perfect marriage, because sin had not yet polluted everything.

> *The reason people give sex away so easily is that they don't know how valuable sexual purity is in God's eyes.*

But even the entrance of sin did not change God's sexual standards. God's sexual norm outside of marriage is virginity, an extremely valuable gift from Him that you can give away only once and never get back again. But if you're reading this and have already committed sexual sin, please don't stop reading this chapter. The principles we learn in John 8, where a woman was caught in adultery, ought to encourage you to put the past behind you and move forward.

While others wanted to judge the woman for her sexual sin, Jesus dismissed them and told them to go away, because they were equally guilty of the same or similar sins themselves. Not only did He remove the accusers, but He also removed the condemnation the woman felt. He forgave her sins, removed her condemnation, and told her she could go in peace. He also told her to go and sin no more.

The key is in knowing that in Christ, you are not condemned when you repent of your sins. Repentance is making the internal determination and resolve to turn from your sins, accompanied by visible changes in your actions (i.e., fruits of repentance). And repentance also means you are able to move forward in your life and sin no more in this area of sexuality, even though temptations will continue to come. As a kingdom single who has committed yourself to fully and freely maximizing your completeness under the rule of God and lordship of Jesus Christ, even your sexuality must operate under His authority. Remember, a diamond that has gotten dirty is still a valuable jewel. It just needs to be cleaned and polished so it can recapture its original beauty and glory.

Corinthian Chaos

The church at Corinth had sexual problems. The Corinthians lived in a sex-obsessed city, a port city that welcomed ships from all over. Corinth was the New York or the Los Angeles of its day. It was the place to be, built to service all this activity and all the merchants and sailors who came around.

In fact, on a hill in Corinth sat the *Ico-Corinthus,* the temple of Aphrodite, the goddess of love. This temple was divided in half—one side was a restaurant, and the other side was a brothel. People would go to the restaurant for dinner and to the brothel for "dessert." Essentially, the brothel was made up of rooms that housed a thousand or more "sacred" prostitutes who engaged in sex with worshipers as part of their pagan rites.

Because of that, Paul had to explain in his first letter to this church that having sex is not the same as having dinner. The people in Corinth were misguided about sex, because their attitude was that sex was like food. When you get hungry, you eat. When your body craves sex, you do the same thing with your sexual drive that you do with your hunger. You satisfy it.

But Paul had a word for them, and it's a word for us as well. Yet before addressing the difference between food and sex, Paul made an important point about sexual passion in general when he said, "All things are lawful for me, but not all things are profitable. All things are lawful for me, but I will not be mastered by anything" (1 Corinthians 6:12). In other words, God has rules that govern how we use what we have been given.

> *Freedom does not mean doing whatever you* want *to do. Freedom is doing what you* ought *to do.*

Sex is a legitimate and lawful passion given to us by God. So if you're struggling sexually, you don't pray that God will take away your sexual passion. You are then asking not to be human. You pray that you not be mastered by your legitimate and lawful sexual passion so that the expression of it becomes your obsession, no matter what God's rules say. Sex is part of your God-given DNA, but it was never designed to be your master.

You see, freedom does not mean doing whatever you *want* to do. Freedom is doing what you *ought* to do.

Suppose a man stands on top of a tall building and says, "I want to be free from gravity. I am going to do my own thing. So let me serve notice on you, gravity. I am in charge now. I am free." He jumps off the building, and for a couple seconds he's free. But it doesn't take long for it to dawn on him that he's not as free as he thought. That is confirmed as he's swept off the pavement below. Gravity was in charge all along.

Sex is like a fire. Contained in the fireplace, a fire keeps everybody warm. Set the fire free, though, and the whole house burns. You don't want the fire in your house to be free of boundaries. You want it contained so that it's free to generate warmth and not destruction.

And while sex is like a fire, it's not like food—a major distinction Paul needed to draw for the Corinthians. Paul noted this difference in the very next verse, where he said, "Food is for the stomach and the stomach is for food, but God will do away with both of them. Yet the body is not for immorality, but for the Lord, and the Lord is for the body" (1 Corinthians 6:13).

When you get hungry, it's okay to eat because God has designed the stomach to receive the food. There's no great issue involved, because someday both food and your stomach will be obsolete. But sex cannot be equated with food—there is much more at stake. God didn't put us on Earth so we could indulge our sexual passions. We're to use our bodies—that is, our lives—to glorify Him.

But someone might say, "Everybody else is doing it." God's answer is, "Since when are you everybody else? Since when does the crowd dictate what you're supposed to do?"

Large supermarkets these days have sampling stations where people can taste what the store has to offer. Some people make full meals visiting these areas without committing to purchase the products they've tested. Unfortunately, and even especially in the church these days, far too many men use women as tasting stations. They go from person to person to satisfy their hunger, without making a commitment to anyone.

Males in particular who desire to be a kingdom single should stop this practice immediately. And women who desire to be a kingdom single should no longer allow themselves to be used by men who are simply seeking to satisfy their desires.

Desire in and of itself is not the issue. It's in managing that desire (or having that desire manage you) that the issue arises. Many Christians today struggle with sexual sin just as the Corinthians did. We're all susceptible to it. It all stems from the same root—our sinful flesh, nurtured by a secular worldview that causes us believers to be governed by what the culture says and not by who we are in Christ.

So the question is not whether we have a sexual appetite. The question is, what legitimate avenue has God given us through which to satisfy that appetite? It's only in marriage. Unless you start with this mentality, you're going to believe and act on the lie that you're free to have sex whenever you feel like it. You're going to buy into the thinking that "this is just the way God made me."

Another difference between food and sex is that what you eat does not equate into what happens in eternity, but sex does. In fact, your morality affects your inheritance in eternity. We read, "Neither the sexually immoral . . . nor adulterers nor men who have sex with men . . . will inherit the kingdom of God" (1 Corinthians 6:9-10, NIV). Paul states clearly in this passage that your sexual immorality will affect your inheritance in the kingdom of God. It will affect what you receive when you stand before Christ and He offers you your reward.

Let's look again at what Paul wrote in 1 Corinthians 6:

> Do you not know that your bodies are members of Christ? Shall I
> then take away the members of Christ and make them members of a
> prostitute? May it never be! Or do you not know that the one who
> joins himself to a prostitute is one body with her? For He says, "The
> two shall become one flesh." But the one who joins himself to the
> Lord is one spirit with Him. (1 Corinthians 6:15-17)

The believers in Corinth were part of a pagan Greek world that taught a two-tiered view of the universe. The Greeks believed that the spiritual and the physical were on two completely separate levels. Therefore, you could do what you wanted with your body and not affect your spirit.

God says no to that view. The body and the spirit are closely linked. For the Christian, sex is a spiritual issue. You cannot worship God on Sunday, enter into sexual immorality on Monday, and keep those separate, because your body, and not just your spirit, is for the Lord. In fact, as a Christian, any time you engage in sexual activities, whether physically or even mentally, Christ is right there with you.

Like a pregnant woman who abuses drugs, thus making her baby an involuntary participant in her drug habit, when you engage in sexual immorality as a child of the King, you make Jesus an involuntary participant in what you're doing.

> *For the Christian,*
> *sex is a spiritual issue.*

As a Christian, you have been bought with a very high price—the death and blood of Jesus Christ. You are no longer yours. You are owned by Christ, "For you have been bought with a price: therefore glorify God in your body" (1 Corinthians 6:20). Your body is now the temple of the Holy Spirit, which means that every time you have sex or engage in sexual activities, physically or mentally, you go to church.

The temple was a place of worship, so fundamentally what you're saying is, "Let's have a worship service right now." The next time you think about engaging in immoral sex, ask yourself if that is something you would do in the sanctuary. Because that's what you're doing. Your body is the sanctuary of the Holy Spirit.

Likewise, in these verses, Paul tells us there is no biblical view of sex without commitment. The only lawful use of sex is within marriage, where two become one. You don't have sex in order to have commitment. You make a commitment first, and then you celebrate it with sex. You don't say, "Let's try it, and then I'll see whether I want to marry you."

No. You marry, and then you try it. Women, don't get played by smooth-talking men who want to show you love without committing to the love they want to show you. Why? Because you're more valuable than that. You're too valuable to be a party favor of immature men who only want to gratify their libidos.

Instead, hold your head up high and declare your value. Ask him, "Are you willing to put your life on the line for me?" Buying you dinner and a movie is not a commitment. But when you enter a lifetime commitment, that's when you are to express your sexuality together.

And I understand this is often difficult to discern. I've heard this more than once from singles: "At least with worldly dudes you know what you're getting. Christian men will use holiness as a marketing tool that we want to believe, only to see they're no different. Sure, sex may be meant for marriage, but many times unbelieving dudes are more straightforward and treat me better than Christian guys." So just because he's Christian—or just because she's Christian—that doesn't mean much when it comes to singles and sex. Keep your guard up and your personal boundaries high.

Paul is not saying that sex outside of marriage is wrong simply because two warm bodies come together. Something much more significant is happening. Sex outside of marriage is the ultimate lie, because two people are performing the act of marriage without the covenant. No such thing was ever intended in God's economy.

Many people, even believers, who have been married for a long time are still suffering from the scars resulting from activities earlier in their lives, perhaps in their teenage years. There is no other sin quite like sexual sin, because every other sin is external in its effect. But immorality does damage to the soul.

Why? Because, as we've seen, Paul says that when you engage in physical intimacy, that engagement produces a new thing. The two people become one. There is no other realm, other than when you are joined to Christ in salvation, where this kind of intimacy happens. Not only that, but there are also chemical imprints being made in your brain that solidify the connection of sex. It's like taking sodium and matching it with chloride. You wind up with salt, which is something brand-new. In the same way, when you mix two parts hydrogen with one part oxygen, you get water. When you bring two people together through the sexual relationship, Scripture says you wind up with something brand-new.

Now, if you decide you don't want the new thing you just created—if it was just a momentary passion or a fling—then you break it apart. But in the breaking apart, you tear away a piece of yourself. Obviously, the more times you do this, the more withdrawal you experience and the greater the loss you feel.

Anyone who has kids knows what it's like to try to get chewing gum out of the carpet, especially after someone has stepped on it. It's challenging to try to pull that gum out without leaving any behind. The merger of the gum with the fiber in the carpet has so integrated them that to get out all the gum, you have to tear away some of the carpet, too. And you usually leave some of the gum behind anyway.

So it is when there's a merger of two people in sexual intercourse. When they try to tear that relationship apart, they tear themselves, and a part of them is left behind as well.

You say, "Tony, this is tough. I want to maintain my purity, but sex is all around me. What do I do?" Paul has a two-word answer for you: "Flee immorality" (1 Corinthians 6:18). In other words, run! Get out of there. Move your feet. Aim ahead of the temptation. Be out in front of it with boundaries and coping techniques.

You can't emotionalize, theorize, or play with sexual temptation. You have to hit the track and get out of there. You cannot keep placing yourself in environments that are sexually tempting and expect to stay clean. This may mean changing your viewing and reading habits, your dating habits, or even your friends.

Go back to 1 Corinthians 6 and look at the rest of verse 18 again:

"Every other sin that a man commits is outside the body, but the immoral man sins against his own body." There it is. When you develop a lifestyle of immorality, it is unlike any other sin in its destructive nature.

Drugs can't compare with sex in its destructiveness. Crime can't compare with it. Nothing can compare with it, because sexual sin carries its own built-in, self-deteriorating mechanism. Why? Because of what we said above: Sex uniquely combines the physical and the spiritual.

The act of sex means that a spiritual relationship has taken place. So when it's an illegitimate spiritual relationship and you back out of it, you back out with spiritual as well as physical and emotional damage. Many people don't even know that this is what they're battling in their marriages—the holdover from things that happened earlier but have never been dealt with. Immorality is uniquely used by Satan and his demons to advance his evil, rival kingdom against God while simultaneously bringing spiritual and social consequences to mankind (Genesis 6:1-13).

> *Immorality is like a cat's paw. When lightly stroked, it's soft and pleasurable. But increased pressure brings out the claws of sin that will shred your very life.*

Immorality is like a cat's paw. When lightly stroked, it's soft and pleasurable. But increased pressure brings out the claws of sin that will shred your very life. The immoral person is like a man who robs a bank and gets what he wants for the moment, but then has to pay the price for a lifetime once he's caught. However, the morally pure person is like a bank depositor who puts his money away where it is securely held as the interest builds up, so that he can really enjoy it when it's time to draw on his account.

What we are seeing in our world today is the destruction being wrought by men and women who have taken God's idea of sex and contaminated it. God places a great deal of value on virginity and sexual purity.

Kingdom single, since this is not the message your culture is giving you, you in particular are going to have to be countercultural. You're going to have to go against the crowd. Paul did not skip the subject of sexual morality, because he couldn't. He lived in a decrepit world full of incest, debauchery, and prostitution. His world was morally contaminated, and these Christians at Corinth, and I'm sure in other places, had all kinds of questions: How do I control myself in a world like this? What should my attitude toward marriage be?

Sounds familiar, doesn't it? What we're facing is nothing new. Divorce was common in the New Testament world. In fact, in Paul's day it was not uncommon for someone to have been married twenty times. A man could get rid of his wife for almost any reason: She couldn't cook, she was getting a little overweight, the wrinkles were starting to come—wrinkles the husband had no doubt caused. Nevertheless, all these ridiculous things became grounds for divorce.

Paul stepped into this madness to tell Christians they had to go against the culture. As we saw earlier, he argued that God created sexuality, and therefore He must define it. Any definition of sexuality that leaves God out is a defective definition—and a destructive one.

So the immoral person sins against his own body. That is, when we engage in immorality, we start to self-destruct. There's no area of life that can bring such internal damage as this one, Paul says.

Don't Light the Fire

Paul has a word for single people and married couples as in chapter 7 of his first letter to the Corinthians he transitions to answering questions they had written to him. He gets right to the heart of the matter in verse 1: "It is good for a man not to touch a woman." That word *touch* means "to light a fire," which came to be understood as a euphemism for sexual passion and activity. Paul says that it's good if that fire is not lit because, once it's lit, it's very hard to extinguish. And, once it's lit, that fire can easily burn out of control.

Since Paul says it's good not to light the fire of sexual passion, the Bible's word to singles is that your singleness can never be good unless it is celibate.

If you're single and acting as if you're married—that is, if you're unmarried but are physically involved with another person so that you're functioning as married people—that is not good. Your singleness will never be good under God until it is a chaste singleness. If you're trying to live in two worlds at one time, you will never know the good and God-honoring single life Paul talks about. In fact, Paul speaks so favorably of singleness that he says, "I wish that all men were [unmarried] even as I myself am" (1 Corinthians 7:7).

Singles, if you really want to maximize your singleness, it's good to avoid lighting the fire of sexual passion, to abstain from immorality. Then God will bless and maximize your singleness, and you will find the fulfillment, meaning, and direction He wants you to have.

So Paul says that to avoid immorality, men and women must save themselves for marriage. The fact is that some people were so sexually active *before* they got married that they were running on low octane *after* they got married. Their passions burned too early, and now they had burned low because they didn't keep what was special and sacred for the marriage bed. This helps to explain the high sales of Viagra and other performance-enhancing drugs.

Young woman, don't let any player tell you that because he washed his car, got his hair cut, got all shined up, took you out, and spent all his money on you, he's done his job. And now it's time for you to be the party favor. Tell him to forget it. He can't make sexual advances on you just because he did any of those things. He can take his money and go home. Tell him good-bye.

Why? Because you're not for sale. Remember, after the intimacy, when he walks away, he takes part of you with him and leaves part of himself imprinted on you. Outside of marriage, you have no sexual obligation just because a guy is nice. Until he's willing to give *all* of himself to you, he can demand nothing from you.

If he says, "If you loved me, you would," you say, "Because I love God more, I won't." In fact, God explicitly instructs men not to touch (ignite spiritual passion) a woman to whom they're not married (1 Corinthians 7:1-2). A man cannot be a player and a kingdom man at the same time. Rather, single men should honor and protect the purity and emotional well-being of their single sisters.

God's idea is that the sexual relationship is to be preserved for one man and one woman in the context of marriage. Sex is not a way to say thank you for a nice evening. Sex was not given for you to release tension or explore a hobby. Sex was not given just so you can feel good. It was given to express your total commitment to another person within the covenant of marriage.

Sex is not a way to say thank you for a nice evening.

It's a very serious thing to unleash one's sexuality outside the safety of a lifelong, one-flesh marriage. Marriage is God's only method for safe sex.

I've lived long enough to know that a large number of singles reading this book have already had sex outside marriage. And while you can never go back and undo what's been done, I want to remind you and encourage you to consider the importance of preserving your sexual purity and spiritual virtue from this day forward. When this decision is made, you will hear the restorative words of Jesus, "Neither do I condemn you, go and sin no more."

This applies to men and women equally. It's important to note that Jesus rejected the group of male accusers who sought to destroy the life of the woman caught in immorality. He rejected their moral hypocrisy, as well as their failure to hold accountable the man who was also a participant in the sin (John 8:1-11).

Every community has a local dry cleaner. This is where people bring their dirty clothes to get them cleaned. My local cleaner is just down the road a couple of blocks, and most Wednesdays you'll find me dropping something off and picking up something else. It's amazing how what I drop off is transformed into something brand-new when I pick it up.

Friend, Jesus has a cleaning service, too. He would be delighted to receive your past mistakes and the sins you've committed sexually, clean you up, and give your sexuality back to you fresh and new again. That's how you can reclaim your spiritual purity. And just as many cleaners have a tailor as well, Jesus can also stitch together that which has been torn or tattered when you bring your past to Him through repentance. He can make you new again and restore your divine dignity and your renewed status as a kingdom single.

There are so many levels to sexual purity, though, to consider. It has multiple layers, angles, and areas and goes beyond intercourse itself. One question I've had come up over the years is, "I don't know if I can go forever and not scratch the itch. It's unfair that I live and work to express holiness, and God has chosen not to answer this prayer. What can I do in the meantime?" Of course, the question largely revolves around masturbation. While the Bible never comments directly on masturbation or physical release, it does comment on the issue of illegitimate mental thoughts and lust. So whenever the two get connected—that is, illegitimate mental thoughts with physical release—then the physical release becomes illegitimate.

That then raises the next question: Is masturbation not a sin if unaccompanied by illegitimate thoughts or lust? Most of us are aware that physical release can happen without the aid of thoughts or lust. When or if that's the case, then sin has not occurred. The greater issue in masturbation is that of lust and sinful thoughts.

As masturbation progresses, though, you are setting yourself up to be inviting those thoughts, whether you intended to at the beginning or not. Thus, you are essentially playing with fire. Each person knows what it takes to create his or her own physical release and how dependent he or she is on lust or illegitimate thoughts to go with it, so the answer to this question is personal for each individual.

But ultimately, lust is a sin, and masturbation is difficult to do without it (for most people). In addition, just as marijuana is a "gateway" drug to deeper strongholds and harsher drugs, so also masturbation often serves as a gateway to deeper, illegitimate areas of sexual satisfaction.

Based on that reality, I would recommend looking for alternative ways of discovering pleasure in your life as a single or releasing pent-up emotions, physical feelings, and desires. Some alternatives might include running, exercise programs, dance (Zumba, modern, or competitive dance), sports, singing (whether alone or publicly), playing an instrument, painting, volunteering at your local pet rescue center, or other activities that engage your emotions, burn energy, and/or give you a sense of fulfillment.

Mourning Your Virginity or Singleness

Recently I sat across from a middle-aged woman who had never been married and had remained a virgin. "Pastor," she said, her voice hesitant yet sure at the same time, "is it okay if I mourn my virginity?" The question seemed valid, and it was one I had never been asked before. My mind quickly raced to Judges chapter 11 and the story of Jephthah, who had made an unwise vow to sacrifice to God whatever came through the door of his home first, if God would give him victory over his enemies.

To his chagrin, instead of an animal coming out his door first, it was his only daughter. This meant she would have to give up her personal hope for sexual fulfillment, marriage, and children in order to complete her father's pledge. Because of her own commitment to God and her father, she submitted to the vow to be given to the Lord for a lifetime of service.

But something interesting happened before she did. It's something rarely preached on or taught, but its significance for singles cannot be overstated. Prior to surrendering her life to the Lord's service, she requested permission to have a period of time when she could mourn the loss of a future marriage, sexuality, and a family. Essentially, she asked to mourn her virginity.

We read about her very touching and personal story at the end of the chapter:

> So she said to him, "My father, you have given your word to the LORD; do to me as you have said, since the LORD has avenged you of your enemies, the sons of Ammon." She said to her father, "Let this thing be done for me; let me alone two months, that I may go to the mountains and weep because of my virginity, I and my companions." Then he said, "Go." So he sent her away for two months; and she left with her companions, and wept on the mountains because of her virginity. At the end of two months she returned to her father, who did to her according to the vow which he had made; and she had no relations with a man. Thus it became a custom in Israel, that the daughters of Israel went yearly to commemorate the daughter of Jephthah the Gileadite four days in the year. (Judges 11:36-40)

So great was the sacrifice of keeping her virginity that even after she returned, the women of Israel made an annual trip for four days to commemorate what she had given up. If this passage doesn't speak to the depth of loss that many singles face, nothing else ever could. To make light of or brush over the losses that singleness includes is to be naïve to our makeup as relational beings made in the image of a relational God.

My answer to the woman sitting across from me in the counseling session was an unabashed "Yes." Yes, to mourn your virginity is a healthy process for reconciling yourself to the loss that is so prevalent in life. What is unhealthy is to carry that sadness and need for physical, relational, and even often parental fulfillment throughout each and every day. That attitude creates a cloud cover under which you must live, thus reducing your capacity for joy, peace, and satisfaction in life. To mourn as the woman did in Judges 11 is to set aside a time and space where grief can be processed. And once it's processed, to pick up the pieces and move on.

Yet unfortunately the mourning of loss for singles in our culture today is elongated because, first of all, no one speaks of the importance of grieving. And second, married Christians often make things worse for singles with questions like, "When are you going to get married?" or insensitive statements like, "Remember, you're married to God."

In addition, the church is also guilty of making things worse by not celebrating singleness the way we celebrate marriage and family. This reinforces a feeling of a spiritual second-class citizenship among singles, thus increasing both the intensity and longevity of the mourning.

The church is guilty of making things worse by not celebrating singleness the way we celebrate marriage and family.

The story of Jephthah's daughter tells us it's okay for kingdom singles to mourn their virginity and their singleness. That is, it's okay to honestly express their sadness to God over the sense of loss they feel at the absence of sexual fulfillment, marriage, and children. Jephthah's daughter made it clear that it was her commitment to God and respect for her father that were the foundation of her mourning (Judges 11:36).

However, while it's okay to visit your state of mourning, it's not okay to wallow in it. Jephthah's daughter took a two-month sabbatical to come to grips with her spiritual reality. After that, she visited her status only four days a year (Judges 11:40). It should also be noted that she didn't mourn alone. She had friends who lamented with her. Friend, even though you're single, you are not to be alone (verses 38, 40).

Once her mourning period was over, she spent the rest of her time in kingdom work, devoted to the Lord. So if you're mourning your virginity or singleness because of your unwillingness to compromise your spiritual values and commitment, please know that this is a healthy approach to processing your emotions and loss, as long as you just visit the mountain of mourning and don't choose to live there.

Instead, live in the service of God, maximizing your kingdom impact.

12

∽◦∾

SINGLES AND SEX,
PART 2

The December air greeted us with a chilly embrace as we made our way out of the house, down the hill in the backyard, and across the field. Having grown up in urban Baltimore, where concrete was far more prevalent than trees, I had definitely stepped into a foreign environment.

Lois and I were in the middle of enjoying a Christmas getaway with some close friends who lived in a rural area. But on this Christmas, we got much more than the normal holiday brunch and shared conversations. On this trip, I got a lesson in skeet shooting as well.

Now, anyone who knows me knows that skeet shooting and Tony Evans aren't exactly best friends. In fact, prior to this event, I can't recall ever even picking up a gun. I'm a sports man. As the chaplain for both the NBA's Dallas Mavericks and the NFL's Dallas Cowboys, I get to regularly witness competitive sports that involve hand-to-hand contact—or at least body-to-body from time to time. As a former football player myself, I like my recreational activities to include sweat, guts, and sheer force.

The idea of holding a gun, pulling a trigger, and watching a clay target possibly break into pieces didn't do much for me. But as the polite and grateful guest that I am, I went along for the supposed adventure. Anyhow, who doesn't love a challenge? Certainly I could knock those clay birds out of the sky like the best of them.

Wrong.

The first clay bird flew. I aimed. Shot. Got nothing.

Then the next one flew, and I aimed again. Still nothing.

And again. Nothing.

Again. Nothing.

Now, even though the years may have matured me, my vision is still 20/20. And my hands are still steady. I had seen the object in the air. I had aimed. I had pulled the trigger. Yet the clay birds just kept flying.

After a few too many flew away and my friend no doubt saw the perplexity come over my face, he walked over to me and said, "Tony . . . ." Placing his hand on my shoulder, he proceeded to explain both the art and science of skeet shooting. "Tony," he said my name again. I think he wanted me to make sure and listen closely. "The clay object is like a bird. When it's released, it's flying across the sky just like a bird. It's moving. So if you want to shoot it out of the sky, you can't aim at it. If you aim at it, by the time your pellets get there, it will be long gone. In order to shoot the skeet out of the sky, you have to get in front of it. You have to be ahead of it. Your aim must always go before it."

I took my friend's wisdom and decided to apply it. He made sense. So I regrouped and called out, "Pull."

Up flew the clay bird.

This time I squeezed the trigger while aiming out in front of it.

BAM!

That bird was destroyed! Obliterated. Pieces of it rained down from the sky.

Now, you may be wondering what skeet shooting has to do with sex. A lot, actually. Because how you handle yourself sexually, or fail to handle yourself, will have everything to do with where you aim. You must get out in front of it. If you think that it's something you can decide on in the heat of the moment, that bird will fly. If you think you can decide where that so-called "invisible line" is that you won't cross when you reach it, that bird will fly. If you choose to dabble here or dabble there in sexually explicit television shows, music, movies, or porn, that bird is going to fly.

A recent study showed that teens who watch a high level of programming with sexual content were twice as likely to get pregnant over the next three years as those who didn't.[1] What we view affects what we do. Guard your eyes and you will guard your actions.

> *What we view affects what we do. Guard your eyes and you will guard your actions.*

As a single, the only way to successfully handle the power and force of this dynamism called *sex* is to go out before it. You must draw your boundaries before having to use them. You must choose to outwit it and "out aim" it. You must understand it. Take charge over it. And, most importantly, always be in front of it.

Yada and You

I found one of the most revealing principles about sexuality I ever discovered in the Bible when I was preparing to preach on an entirely different subject. A few years back, in the middle of studying for and getting ready to dive into a twelve-week series on the subject of knowing God, I came across a powerful reality about sex.

In fact, so powerful was this truth that it became the backdrop for illustrating throughout the entire series the depth of the relationship God desires to have with each of us. I've touched on it in this book in another chapter. But let's explore it more in the context of intimacy itself.

Sexual intimacy involves far more than merely two bodies experiencing contact and exchanging fluids. If that were all that was required for intimacy to occur, then prostitutes would be the most intimate people in the world.

But in the original Hebrew language of the Old Testament, we discover something incredibly powerful about sexuality. When we uncover the intent of the original language, we learn that sex is designed to involve discovering the depths of another being in such a way as to both *know* and *be known*—much more than mere physical contact, and only attainable in an atmosphere of total and deserved trust.

In accordance with the theological *Law of First Mention*, we see that the first time Scripture mentions sexual intimacy is in Genesis 4:1, where we read, "Now the man *had relations* with his wife Eve, and she conceived and gave birth" (italics mine).

The Hebrew term used in the very first account of sexual intimacy— "had relations"—is the word *yada*.[2] It's the same word used a few verses earlier in saying that Adam and Eve's eyes had been opened and they "knew" they were naked. It's also the same word used when we read, "Then the LORD God said, 'Behold, the man has become like one of Us, *knowing* good and evil'"(Genesis 3:22, italics mine).

The word *yada* does not refer to body parts or physical activity. In all definitions of the word *yada,* which occurs over 900 times in the Old Testament, it means:

- to know, learn to know
- to be made known, be revealed
- to make oneself known
- to cause to know
- to reveal oneself
- to know by experience

Each time *yada* is used in connection with relational interaction, it indicates discovering the depths of another person's reality—or even exploring the depths of the reality of God Himself. In fact, it has the capacity to be so intimate a term when applied to relational involvement that God uses it to refer to His own relationship with us in the absolute closest of interactions:

> The secret of the LORD is for those who fear Him, and He will make them *know* [yada] His covenant. (Psalm 25:14, italics mine)

> "You are My witnesses," declares the LORD, "and My servant whom I have chosen, so that you may *know* [yada] and believe Me." (Isaiah 43:10, italics mine)

> I will give you the treasures of darkness and hidden wealth of secret places, so that you may *know* [yada] that it is I, the LORD, the God of Israel, who calls you by your name. (Isaiah 45:3, italics mine)

In each of these passages, God speaks of His relationship in a close and intimate manner. We read about "treasures of darkness," being "chosen," and God's self-obligatory relationship He establishes called "His covenant." On top of that, twice we read the specific word *secret*—once in reference to God's secrets, "the secret of the LORD," and also in relation to what God will give, "hidden wealth of secret places."

One thing that's always true about secrets is that you have to be pretty close in order to share them. Of course you have to be close intimately by way of trust, but oftentimes that also includes being close in physical proximity.

When you were younger and you wanted to tell someone a secret, what would you normally do? If you were like me, you would get next to the other person—close enough that you could lean over and, with your hand cupped around your mouth, whisper in his or her ear.

That's the typical way of sharing a secret.

And that's what God says He will do with those who know (*yada*) Him. He will be so close that you can hear Him whispering in your ear, telling you the secrets reserved for those who have a special relationship of intimacy with Him.

Yet what is essential to realize is that when God chose to *yada* us, He chose to do so with a people who are perishing (John 3:16), have gone astray (Luke 19:10), and are condemned (John 3:18). God gave the perfection of His *yada* to those who knew only imperfection (Romans 3:23). He revealed the purity of Himself to those who are desperately wicked (Jeremiah 17:9). And He was able to do all this while maintaining His holiness because Jesus hung on a cross as a sacrifice for the sins of us all. Jesus not only died, but He also died to Himself, as we read: "He humbled Himself by becoming obedient to the point of death, even death on a cross" (Philippians 2:8).

Likewise, the very foundation of true *yada* of one another in the security of the marriage union is a sacrificial dying to yourself in such a way that you lay your will, pride, and needs on the altar while considering the other as more important than yourself. It's in this sacrifice, where both partners die to themselves, that what is new can grow and flourish in the soil of biblical love.

> *God revealed the purity of Himself to those who are desperately wicked (Jeremiah 17:9).*

This is because in sacred sex, the two partners share much more than some moments of passion. They share their secrets, their hearts' DNA, their fears, their hopes, their failures, and even so much as their "treasures of darkness and hidden wealth of secret places." They reveal themselves in a way unlike with any other. And within that revelation, if it is truly *yada*, they are to find the most authentic form of love possible.

In fact, the secret nature of what they share becomes its own treasure. Because how do you make a secret no longer a secret?

You tell it to others.

It's the same thing with the sacredness of sex. Sex is no longer a sacred shared experience—it is no longer *yada*—when it's no longer unique between the two who share it. If and when sexual relations become something common—something shared with those other than the ones bound by a *yada* relationship—they change from being what God had originally intended into that which Satan corrupted, known in Scripture as *porneuō*[3] or *shakab*.[4]

Both of these terms refer to the same physical activity as in *yada*, yet both remove the sacred and replace it with the common. Thus, they remove one of the main purposes and intentions of sexuality, the exclusive unveiling of knowing and being known.

And when this is done, as we see repeatedly through Scripture, the results are heartbreak, jealousy, regret, and severe emotional, physical, and even spiritual consequences. For example, we do not read *yada* in reference to the following, but rather *shakab*:

- David and Bathsheba
- Tamar's rape by Amnon
- Lot's daughters' sexual activity with him
- Shechem defiling Dinah
- Reuben and his father's concubine
- Even Jacob and the wife he did not love, Leah

A person can engage in physical relations with another person and not experience *yada*—not share the intimate and sacred realities of the depths of who they are. This is not what God had intended when He created the sacred act of sex. This is not how He chose to introduce the concept of sexuality to us in its origin in the Garden.

The primary principle to remember and hold onto in guarding your sexual purity as a kingdom single is God's original intention for sex—as a shared, unveiled revealing involving knowing and being known.

Keep in mind, the very nature of a veil is to keep something hidden or secret. If not, it becomes a scarf or a head wrap, not a veil. Likewise, *yada* can quickly deteriorate into *shakab* or *porneuō*, carrying with it the inevitable outcomes associated with sex in the absence of a sacredly shared trust.

A Covenant

Sex was never designed to simply be a mechanism for biological fulfillment. It was not designed merely to address the problem of raging testosterone or elevated hormones. Sex was designed both to inaugurate a covenant and to renew it.

Consummation of a marriage on the wedding night is designed to inaugurate a covenant. And from that point on, as often as you do it, you renew the covenant and commitment that were inaugurated on the wedding night.

In Scripture, covenants were frequently established by blood. For example, God made a covenant with Abraham, the sign of which was circumcision (Genesis 17:10-12). All the males born in Israel were to come as young boys and have the foreskin of their sexual organ removed to signify that they were part of God's covenant people. They were to be unlike everybody else.

Why was circumcision chosen as the sign of the Abrahamic covenant, which would establish Israel as God's special people and through which Abraham would become the father of many nations? Because this covenant was fulfilled and expanded as Abraham and his male descendants produced children.

Therefore, their sexual organs would bear the mark of the covenant as a special sign that they and the children they fathered were set apart to the Lord. The rite of circumcision involved blood, which was part of the covenant.

So it is in marriage. Look at Deuteronomy 22:13-15:

> If any man takes a wife and goes in to her and then turns against
> her, and charges her with shameful deeds and publicly defames her,
> and says, "I took this woman, but when I came near her, I did not
> find her a virgin," then the girl's father and her mother shall take
> and bring out the evidence of the girl's virginity to the elders of the
> city at the gate.

The evidence was the bloodstained sheet or whatever covering was on
the bed when the couple consummated their marriage on their wedding
night. Read the verses that follow in Deuteronomy 22 and you'll see that if
the parents could prove their daughter's virginity, she was acquitted and the
husband was fined.

But if there was no blood, meaning the woman was not a virgin prior
to her marriage, she could be put to death (Deuteronomy 22:21), because
the covenant of marriage was inaugurated by blood.

God created a shield, the hymen, around a woman's sex organ, designed to cover her until her wedding night, when it is broken and blood is
shed over the male sex organ. This act consummates the covenant of an
unbreakable bond between two people and God. Of course, there are medical and genetic reasons why a woman's hymen may not be in place on her
wedding night, even without previous sex, but the overarching principle
established in the beginning remains.

Chemical Bonds

While a covenant is a spiritual bond between two people and God, the act
of sexual intimacy also creates a physiological bond between two people.
Sex doesn't necessarily take place in the bedroom. Rather, advances in

scientific research have revealed that sex takes place between the ears—in the chemical connections occurring in the limbic portion of the brain.

On a practical level, this connection involves the diencephalon (which contains both the thalamus and hypothalamus parts of the brain). The acts of viewing, hearing, smelling, seeing, cuddling, arousal, and orgasm involve a highly complex mixture of chemicals, each designed to regulate an intended response by our Creator.

Within the boundaries of a marital relationship, these chemicals serve the greater purpose of maintaining commitment, either heightening or lessening territorial responses of a male, fostering an environment for procreation and protection, and encouraging the transition from lovers to parents and back to lovers again, as needed.

cooo

Sex doesn't necessarily take place in the bedroom. Rather, advances in scientific research have revealed that sex takes place between the ears.

cooo

Yet outside the boundaries of a marital relationship, the chemical bonds that are created leave lasting scars, cravings, holes, and even symptoms of withdrawal. However, while science may have only recently come forward with an explanation for why and how sexual relationships create such strong bonds physiologically, and therefore leave such excruciating pain when not cemented in the context of a secure marriage, God's Word has told us this same truth all along.

When Paul wrote to the citizens of Corinth at the height of moral and spiritual decay in that society, his word choice accurately reflected what happens when sex occurs. He said,

> Or do you not know that the one who joins himself to a prostitute
> is one body with her? (1 Corinthians 6:16)

What is most interesting is Paul's use of the word *join*. The original Greek language uses the word *kollaō*.[5] *Kollaō* literally means, "to glue together, cement." Under the inspiration of the Holy Spirit, Paul's letter to the Corinthians was as scientifically sound as any of the articles or studies in the most recent medical and psychological journals of our day.

Sexual activity, and its subsequent release of brain-imprinting and -binding chemicals, literally *glues* or *cements* people together. When it comes time for those two people to part ways, a painful physiological reality occurs—primarily among women, whose limbic system, which houses these chemical stores and grooves, is generally larger than that of men.

What's often worse is that unlike in cases of drug addiction, cigarette smoking, porn, or even alcohol, we rarely validate the extreme physiological suffering that women, and even men, suffer because of illicit sexual relationships gone awry. And because this pain is not addressed, repentance is not called for and healing is not encouraged. Thus, these same women and men often end up right back where they once were, trying again to fill the emptiness or craving with someone new.

This happens because a strong physiological reaction occurs in the brain that is very similar to what happens with drugs, alcohol, or addictive behaviors. And to stop the behavior without going through the steps of forgiveness, healing, empowerment, and freedom from it will often only lead that person right back to what he or she had tried to stop. It would be similar to taking away the favorite brand of beer from an alcoholic and then sending him back into a bar with countless other brands to choose from. Would he have stopped drinking his favorite brand of beer? Yes. But would he have the emotional, physical, and spiritual tools necessary to turn down the opportunity to try another brand on another day? Probably not.

That's why it is important for you as a kingdom single to understand not only the spiritual reasons for maintaining a lifestyle that guards your sexual integrity, but also the physiological reactions and interactions you're dealing with if you have engaged in illicit sex in any form, even if that didn't include going as far as intercourse.

Unless you understand what you're seeking to deal with physiologically in overcoming sexual strongholds or temptations in your life, you will be aiming at the clay bird rather than out in front of it. And, as a result, you will miss your target every time.

The major hormones involved in sexual relations are oxytocin, dopamine, and adrenaline. A number of additional chemicals, or hormones, such as serotonin, testosterone, and estrogen, were created by God in connection with the act of sexuality, with parenting, and with maintaining a long-term relationship. The problems arise when this chemical connection is made outside of a spiritual commitment. The chemicals in and of themselves are not bad—in fact, they're good and bring great pleasure to a marital relationship based on the principles of sexual integrity.

But when the chemicals are connected to the fluctuating ups and downs of broken relationships, they can produce great pain and deep psychological wounds. It would be similar to starting an addiction to heroin and then stopping it cold turkey. The desire, attachment, and craving would remain simply due to the chemical impression made on the brain. If the decision to stop heroin stayed in place, in order to satiate the craving and numb the pain, a replacement addictive chemical producer would be sought. And a cycle of addictive behaviors, or symptoms related to pulling away from addictive behaviors—such as depression, confusion, and irritability—would occur.

In essence, heroin would have made a lasting impression, or groove, in the brain that wouldn't go away simply because the drug is no longer around.

A similar thing happens in a chemical connection such as sex. Pile up enough pain from the cementing and tearing apart and you end up with countless people either turning to sex again to try to alleviate the pain or fill the emptiness, or finding other forms of coping, such as overindulgence, spending, alcohol, overworking, drugs, or other addictive behaviors.

Keep in mind that oxytocin can be produced through something as simple as engaged eye contact, subtle touching, and hugs. Again, this is good, when managed. Oxytocin is a positive chemical God gave us to bring happiness and solidify connection in our lives and relationships. Only when high levels of oxytocin belong to an illegitimate attachment to someone you are not married to do they become damaging in the long run. Especially when that relationship either ends or proximity dissipates it over time.

Because once that chemical is present and cemented on the brain, it is difficult to forget it, dismiss it, or satisfy it legitimately outside of marriage.

God's teaching on the sacredness of sex and the essential nature of keeping the sexual relationship pure between two married people joined by covenantal commitment is nothing to take lightly. Knowing how deeply addictive, gluing, and cementing the sexual relationship is, God gives us His warning clearly: "Flee immorality. Every other sin

Oxytocin is a positive chemical God gave us to bring happiness and solidify connection in our lives and relationships.

that a man commits is outside the body, but the immoral man sins against his own body." The immoral person actually sins against his or her own brain, not to mention against his or her own body, in light of all the potential diseases and damage that can be done physically or spiritually.

When sex is kept sacred—when it is a *yada* relationship between two covenanted parties in marriage—it opens up the pathway toward true intimacy and knowing. Yet when sex is casually misused, it creates cemented bonds that, when broken, leave the lingering symptoms of insecurity, pain, abandonment, disrespect for both self and others, and increased neediness for another attachment—making personal relational boundaries likely to be less utilized in future relationships as well.

Paul's warning to the Corinthians to not join (*kollaō*) oneself with another in an immoral relationship is a warning to all kingdom singles today. In order to protect the sacred act of sex, you must aim for the standard God has given us in His Word. You must aim ahead for *yada*.

13

Single Again

With the increased numbers of divorces in today's culture, a common question I hear from singles is, "Is it biblically permissible to marry after a divorce?" I go deeper into this topic in my booklet Divorce and Remarriage, but I want to touch on it here to lay the framework for understanding how to view remarriage.

The Bible says in 1 Corinthians 7:39, "A wife is bound as long as her husband lives; but if her husband is dead, she is free to be married to whom she wishes, only in the Lord." Thus, the Bible only grants freedom from a marriage when the death of a spouse occurs. Now, let me add that the Bible recognizes two kinds of death that can end a marriage. The first and most obvious is physical death, which clearly sets the living partner free from the marriage. There's no disagreement here, so we can move on to the issue of spiritual death.

When God warned Adam not to eat from the forbidden tree, He said, "In the day that you eat from it you will surely die" (Genesis 2:17). Now, the day Adam and Eve ate the fruit, they did not drop dead physically, but they did die spiritually, and their relationship with God was broken.

The Bible recognizes the reality of spiritual death and the separation it brings in a relationship. Jesus said divorce was wrong "except for immorality" (Matthew 19:9), which brings death to a marriage. The Bible says that when there is sexual immorality, which is a form of spiritual death, the marriage dies. There can be forgiveness and restoration, but immorality clearly introduces spiritual death into a marriage.

But the Word does not limit spiritual death to immorality within a marriage. The apostle Paul also wrote of abandonment by an unbelieving spouse (1 Corinthians 7:13-15).

So how can we determine if a marriage is dead and a divorce can be granted without violating God's Word? My counsel is that spouses considering a divorce go to the leadership of their Bible-believing churches and ask them to validate the nature and legitimacy of the grounds for such an action. The death must be recognized by the church, which pronounces that the union is dead and issues the death certificate. In the case of the incestuous man in 1 Corinthians 5, the church should have judged him, because the church is God's court and God's coroner to determine if a death has occurred.

The point of 1 Corinthians 6 is that the church is to act on God's behalf in matters that we normally take to the judge downtown. The church court should be a believer's first court of appeal in a dispute. If a married person believes his or her marriage is spiritually dead, that person should appeal to the church for a judgment. Our church in Dallas holds a church court every week to deal with such matters (verses 1-4).

In the case of marriage and divorce, the problem is that many people don't want to go to the church court because it's too tough. They want to go downtown, where it's easy to get a no-fault divorce. But God doesn't recognize a divorce between believers until the church recognizes that spiritual death exists in the marriage, that one partner has been unfaithful or has developed a totally rebellious, unrepentant attitude (Matthew 18:15-18; 1 Corinthians 6:1-6).

I realize this is more involved than we can discuss fully in this brief context. But I want you to see that it takes a physical or spiritual death to dissolve a marriage and set a person free to marry again. If you're divorced, and your mate has remarried or has entered into an intimate relationship with another person, then you are free to remarry. If your former spouse wishes to reconcile, you should seek to do so if at all possible. If it's not possible, then you should get your church to provide you a certificate of divorce, thus freeing you to remarry, but only in the Lord.

You may be wondering why this divorce issue is such a big deal. Let me encourage you to read Malachi 2:14-16, in which God told the people of Israel that He hated divorce and that because they were divorcing their mates illegitimately, He would not hear their prayers. Anyone who divorces for the wrong reasons leaves God standing at the altar too, because He says He won't listen to that person.

When a death has occurred in the marriage, however, the remaining spouse is free to remarry, but only "in the Lord" (1 Corinthians 7:39; Romans 7:1-3). There is freedom of choice within that boundary.

Married in the Lord

What does it mean to be married in the Lord? Two concepts are at work here. The first is the stipulation that the person being considered for marriage needs to be a Christian. A believer and an unbeliever are never to be joined in any close coequal partnership, including marriage. The Bible says this in 2 Corinthians 6:14-15, where Paul warned, "Do not be bound together with unbelievers; for what partnership have righteousness and lawlessness, or what fellowship has light with darkness? Or what harmony has Christ with Belial, or what has a believer in common with an unbeliever?"

This concept actually comes from Deuteronomy 22:10, where God told Israel not to put an ox and a donkey together in the same yoke because they're different animals that won't be pulling together. They were not created to work together.

This is the picture of a Christian and a non-Christian joining together in marriage. They will not be pulling together equally, and they are going to have problems.

Earlier in this book, I used the example of a single man and a single woman meeting at the airport. It's relevant here as well. The two of them began talking and really started to click with each other. Something was happening; a fire was starting to ignite.

Finally, the man asked the woman where she was flying to. It turned out she was flying south to Florida, while he was flying north to Canada. He wanted the two of them to fly together, but it was impossible because they were going in opposite directions.

If you're a Christian, you're heading in the opposite direction from an unbeliever, and the two of you can't be yoked together without someone getting hurt. This is one area where far too many Christian singles are willing to compromise in order to get married. But the Bible forbids marriage between a believer and a lost person under any circumstance. As someone has said, if you marry a child of the devil, you're going to have in-law problems.

> *If you're a Christian, you're heading in the opposite direction from an unbeliever, and the two of you can't be yoked together without someone getting hurt.*

To be married "only in the Lord" means you are not supposed to marry an unbeliever.

The idea of marrying in the Lord and being equally joined with another Christian also means more than just two people being saved and going to church. You should not only marry a Christian, but it should also be a Christian who is pulling in the same direction as you. It's one thing to marry a Christian, but it's another thing to marry a Christian whose spiritual desires and commitments complement and do not contradict yours.

For example, if you're committed to growing in your faith and you're moving in that direction, you're going to want someone who also wants to grow in Christ.

Let's say you have a desire to serve on the mission field, and you meet another Christian who has no inkling at all that God is calling him or her to the mission field. This difference ought to cause the two of you to go very slowly in your relationship. Otherwise, you may wind up pulling in different directions.

This approach doesn't mean, however, that two people who want to get married must be alike in everything. That will never happen in the first place, and if it did, they would be in for a very boring relationship. But it's important that their differences are at least in the same direction.

Better Off Single

So the desire for marriage is legitimate. But Paul concluded his extended teaching on this subject by saying, "In my opinion she [a widow] is happier if she remains as she is; and I think that I also have the Spirit of God" (1 Corinthians 7:40). This was not just a human opinion, but the revealed Word and will of God. In other words, Paul wasn't just telling his personal bias; he was speaking under the Spirit's inspiration.

Under the Spirit's direction, Paul literally states that a woman is "happier" if she remains single. Essentially, he says, "If she wants to get married, fine—that's her call. But only if she marries in the Lord. Keep in mind, though, girlfriend is going to be happier if she stays single."

Ladies, understand that if you want to get married, you're actually giving up some happiness. If you could only spend a moment listening in on what many married couples go through just on the ride home from church, you might think twice about wanting to get married. Sure, they could look all lovey-dovey dressed up in church, praising the Lord, but the bickering and the fussing sometimes start as early as reaching the pavement of the parking lot.

I'm not saying there's anything wrong with getting married. I'm just saying that Paul, inspired by the Holy Spirit, said you'll be happier if you don't. As a single, you're not in a lesser position; you're in a higher position. You're not in the reduced position; you're in the spiritually exalted position. Why do you think divorce rates are so high and have always been an issue throughout all time? Because married people realize they had it much better in some ways when they were single.

Single Christian—widow, widower, never married, or divorced—my word of counsel to you is this: Don't be in a hurry to get married. Don't rush the process or rush off to the altar with someone who may not be God's choice, simply because you're afraid you may not get another chance. Don't be in such a hurry that you crash and burn.

> *Don't rush the process or rush off to the altar with someone who may not be God's choice, simply because you're afraid you may not get another chance.*

Let me remind you of Ruth, who was a widow and a kingdom single. Ruth determined to pursue God, even if it meant giving up the legitimate pursuit of a husband and the security of marriage. Ruth went to Israel with Naomi, assuming she would never get married again because she was a foreigner from Moab. But as she fulfilled her calling and served the Lord, the day came when she happened to glean in the fields of Boaz—and one of the Bible's great love stories began to unfold.

Ruth was in an obscure position, and humanly speaking she was about as far from having marriage prospects as any woman in her day. But when God was ready, He found her—or rather, He made sure Boaz found her.

But let me point out that the story of Ruth is not the story of a single woman getting married. It's the story of two people who were used of God to carry on the line of the Messiah. Obed, the son born to Ruth and Boaz, was the father of Jesse, who was the father of David, through whom came Jesus Christ! God may have you single right now, but He may also be preparing you for a kingdom purpose much bigger than you could imagine.

Three Choices

Let me give you a helpful formula for approaching the concept of remarriage as a single. If you're free to remarry, you have three choices. Your first choice is to *grumble* about your lot, the lack of suitable potential mates, and the fact that you can feel your biological clock ticking.

A second choice is to *grab* the next available person who comes along, regardless of that person's fitness for marriage. That's a bad choice.

A third choice is to *grow* in grace and in your walk with the Lord. You can say to God, "I am going to walk with You no matter what, and I'm going to trust You and wait on You for Your timing in my life."

What will your choice be? Make sure you make your decision based on your true value and worth, because only then will you be making the right choice.

One day a man was shopping at an antique store where the owner, a woman, had a beautiful table for sale. The price on the table was $600, yet the man thought he would try to get a deal, so he offered her $400 for the table. They began having a conversation about the table, and she informed him that she wouldn't take less than the asking price. The man continued to ask for the discounted price, so the owner began telling him all the unique qualities of this particular table.

Their conversation continued for some time, and then the man asked if she would be willing to take $500.

She said, "No, sir. In fact, we've talked so much about this table that I've been reminded of its true value. As a result, the price is now $1,000."

Unfortunately, today we have far too many single Christians who have forgotten their true value, and so they're willing to reduce themselves cheaply in their decisions, thoughts, and actions. What I hope you will do based on the time we've spent looking at this important subject is to think long, hard, and biblically on your value. When you understand God's view of singleness and how much He cherishes and treasures you, you will hold your head high while living single in His arms and care.

One of the most successful singles in Scripture is Joseph. In spite of the fact that he was born into a dysfunctional family, sold into slavery, falsely accused of rape, and forgotten in prison, the refrain we keep hearing about Joseph is that the Lord was with Him and made him a success, even as a single (Genesis 39:2-3, 21, 23).

He had no partner in his life for more than thirty years, yet he was still successful. The key to his success is that phrase: *the Lord was with him* (Genesis 39:23). But this idea of "with him" was not in a general sense— God's omnipresence, after all, means He's with everybody. Rather, this phrase lets us know that God was specifically with Joseph in a unique manner.

The key to your success as a single is this same phrase. Remember, a kingdom single is *an unmarried Christian who is committed to fully and freely maximizing his or her completeness under the rule of God and the lordship of Jesus Christ.* So if you're single due to abuse, rejection, abandonment, unfaithfulness, or the like, begin the rebuilding process of becoming whole so God can oversee your success.

In other words, the key to single success is your intimate personal relationship with the Lord, and not just a general religious affiliation. There must be a greater focus on that relationship than on the circumstances you're in or the marital status you desire but do not have.

Therefore, during your ups and downs—or the roller coaster of your singleness—make sure you are practicing God's presence daily. Make sure you're putting intimacy with Jesus Christ as your highest priority so that He can make you successful where you are, even in the midst of negative circumstances, knowing that He's using them to take you to your destiny. He's taking you to the place He has for you to glorify Him and to advance His kingdom for the benefit of others.

Negative circumstances during your singleness can seek to push you down and keep you under, but your intimacy with Jesus Christ is like a beach ball being forced underwater. It is only being set up to be propelled higher. Stick close to Jesus as you wait for Him to unfold the fullness of His plan for your life. Once you know your inestimable value as a single, stay connected to the Lord as you wait for Him to change your status.

14

SINGLE PARENTING

My heart was broken recently when the son of a single parent in our church looked up at me and said, "Pastor, why won't God give me a dad? Every night I ask God to give me a dad, but He won't give me one."

What would you have said to him? I didn't have any easy answers for that young man, but I tried to explain that he did have a father, his heavenly Father. Yes, that concept may be beyond his worldview right now, but I wanted him to know he was not alone. And I want to say to you—if you're a single parent—that you're not alone, either. Single parent, God has a word for you, and it's a word of hope and comfort. No matter how you became a single parent, if you love God and have a heart for Him, He is for you.

In Psalm 27:10, David says, "My father and my mother have forsaken me, but the LORD will take me up." David is saying that God will be a parent when a parent is missing. God will take up the slack caused by the absent parent. That's good news. It's good to know your child has a mother you didn't know he or she had, as well as a father if he or she doesn't know where the earthly father is.

David writes in the book of Psalms that God is "a father of the fatherless and a judge for the widows" (Psalm 68:5). If your child does not have a father, that's not the whole story, because God is a Father to the fatherless.

God also acts in justice on behalf of a widow, and widows include those who have been abandoned by a spouse.

The Hebrew word for *orphan* means "fatherless." In Israel, a fatherless child was considered an orphan even if he or she had a mother. Why? Because in the economy of God, it was the father's job to provide for and protect the family. When the father was absent, the family was vulnerable.

In Psalm 146:9, we find more good news for single parents: "The LORD protects the strangers; He supports the fatherless and the widow, but He thwarts the way of the wicked." God supports those who are left alone. He picks up the pieces of their broken lives.

Many people who grew up in single-parent families have seen this truth in action. They made it not because their mothers had a lot to give them but because God showed up in their homes and made the difference. He made a way when there seemed to be no way. He provided when there seemed to be no provision. The fact is, God is so much for the single parent and the child with no dad that it could literally cost someone his life to abuse them:

> You shall not afflict any widow or orphan. If you afflict him at all, and if he does cry out to Me, I will surely hear his cry; and My anger will be kindled, and I will kill you with the sword, and your wives shall become widows and your children fatherless. (Exodus 22:22-24)

God says that you should treat single parents well, because to do otherwise is to place yourself only one step away from that condition yourself. If you're a single parent, this should help you to see how valuable you are. If God will go to your defense at such an extreme level, you should take comfort in His great love for you.

Let me show you one more passage that reveals God's love and care for the single-parent family:

At the end of every third year you shall bring out all the tithe of your produce in that year, and shall deposit it in your town. The Levite, because he has no portion or inheritance among you, and the alien, the orphan and the widow who are in your town, shall come and eat and be satisfied, in order that the LORD your God may bless you in all the work of your hand which you do. (Deuteronomy 14:28-29)

In other words, He was saying that how you treat the fatherless family will often determine how your Father in heaven treats you. How you relate to people who are in need will affect God's hand of goodness on you. Thus, one of the worst things you can do is to spurn people who have not had the opportunities and privileges you've had. You can't know how people ended up in the situation they are in without having walked in their shoes.

It's easy for you as a single parent to feel less valuable than those who come from a nuclear family. Or perhaps you feel out of place when you compare yourself to other families, or you feel as if you're something less worthy or important. Yet God takes special care to mention His great love for those who are vulnerable and alone in trying to raise a family.

The Example of Hagar

If you're a single parent, you have a kindred spirit in Hagar. I call the story of Hagar a saga because it has all the elements of a great drama, and it has some real-life lessons for us as well. We first meet Hagar in Genesis 16, where we learn that she was the servant of Sarai, and that Sarai and Abram (this was just before their names were changed) were unable to have children.

It was the custom of the day in situations like this to bring in another woman who would bear the husband's child and thus act as a surrogate for the barren wife. This was the case with Hagar; Sarai proposed the plan to Abram, who followed her advice.

Now, it's obvious that Sarai wanted a child desperately. But we also need to remember that God had promised her she would bear a child someday. The promise hadn't been fulfilled yet, so, like many of us, Sarai decided to help God out. By her actions she was saying, "Lord, I know Your intentions are good, but since You can't pull this off, let me help You."

Sarai gave Hagar to Abram, and Abram went into Hagar's tent for the purpose of conceiving a child (Genesis 16:4). Bad idea. The plan was doomed from the start, because it was an attempt to bypass God's method and timing and force Him to fulfill His promise.

It was also a bad idea on the human level, because it backfired. When Hagar got pregnant, Sarai felt hurt and jealous. Even though the whole thing was her idea, she said to Abram, "That woman is not staying around here." So in Genesis 16:5-6, Abram and Sarai had an argument about Hagar, and Abram backed down from taking any initiative in the issue. He told her, "Do whatever you want. I'm staying out of this one."

Sarai drove Hagar out of the house, and suddenly Hagar found herself alone and pregnant, with no Abram or any other male to support and protect her. She was about to become a single parent because she got caught in someone else's plan to help God. Many single parents didn't ask for their status. It was brought upon them by someone else's decisions or disobedience, or possibly someone else's persuasion or pressure. But I like verses 7-10 of Genesis 16:

> Now the angel of the LORD found her by a spring of water in the wilderness, by the spring on the way to Shur. He said, "Hagar, Sarai's maid, where have you come from and where are you going?" And she said, "I am fleeing from the presence of my mistress Sarai." Then the angel of the LORD said to her, "Return to your mistress, and submit yourself to her authority." Moreover, the angel of the LORD said to her, "I will greatly multiply your descendants so that they will be too many to count."

The star of the saga arrives: the angel of the Lord. Notice how often it's repeated in just these few verses that it was the angel of the Lord who found Hagar. That's good news when you've been rejected. That's good news when the father of your child is nowhere to be found. That's good news when you find yourself alone and vulnerable.

Who is the angel of the Lord? The Old Testament indicates that He was the revelation of God's presence. Later on, when Abraham was about to sacrifice Isaac, the son he and Sarah had waited for all those years, it was the angel of the Lord who stopped him and said, "Now I know that you fear God, since you have not withheld your son, your only son, from Me" (Genesis 22:12). The angel of the Lord spoke as though He is God, yet He is distinct from God the Father. Who, then, is this divine person who finds Hagar in the wilderness? He is Jesus Christ before His incarnation in Bethlehem.

The angel of the Lord is the preincarnate Son of God. He is the eternal second person of the Godhead. He did not show up for the first time as baby Jesus in a manger in Bethlehem—there is no time when Jesus did not exist. He has always existed, and He made appearances throughout the Old Testament as the angel of the Lord.

If you're a single parent, God knows where you are, the situation you're in, and how you got into the struggles you now face.

What does the angel of the Lord do? He shows up to make things better. Isn't that just like Jesus? He shows up in the Old Testament and in the New Testament. How can He do that? Because He is the same yesterday, today, and forever (Hebrews 13:8). The preincarnate Christ went out to the wilderness for the benefit of a single mother-to-be.

First of all, He found her. If you're a single parent, God knows where you are, the situation you're in, and how you got into the struggles you now face. He loves you, forgives you for wrong choices you may have made, and shows great compassion to you. When you hurt, He feels it. He knows your loneliness, stigma, and pain. After all, He experienced the fullness of all three on the cross.

The Lord told Hagar in Genesis 16:11 that He was very much aware of her condition and very much involved in and interested in the birth of her son. And although Abram did take Hagar as his wife, the context of the passages reveals that Sarai was the wife he loved. In addition, marriage isn't always the case when singles are parents. Many times the child was born outside the bonds of marriage.

Sometimes people call that "illegitimate." But there is no such thing as an illegitimate child, because God has never had a baby that was not legitimate (even if the relationship that produced the offspring was). That is, God has never made a mistake in giving a baby to a set of parents; it is never the case that He didn't mean for that child to be there or considers that child to be any less than a fully valuable human being.

The Bible says in Psalm 139 that every baby is woven together in the womb by God. Whatever the circumstances of a child's conception, the child produced by that relationship is legitimate, because that child bears the image of God.

That ought to be good news for single parents. It doesn't justify wrong actions, but it's an affirmation that God recognizes the value of each life.

Not only did God recognize the life of Hagar's child, but He even named the baby Ishmael (Genesis 16:11). The Hebrew word for this means "God hears." In other words, "God knows what I am going through." Guess what, single parent? God knows. He knows the trouble and stress you're in, and He knows whether it's a situation you got yourself into, someone else put you in, or a combination of both. He also knows where you are right at this very moment.

God showed up in the wilderness and told Hagar what to name her baby. Why is that good? Because every time she ran out of diapers, she could say, "Ishmael needs diapers," for she knew God was listening. When she didn't have enough food to feed Ishmael, his name reminded her that God knew she needed food for her baby. The value of the child is also reflected in the fact that God described details about his future life and personality (Genesis 16:12).

Single parent, God knows what you and your children need. The reason God gave Ishmael his name was so that every time Hagar used it, she would remember something about God. The angel of the Lord told her to call him Ishmael so that every time she spoke his name, she would remember, "God hears and God knows."

That's the beauty of the grace of God for a single parent. Hagar was out on her own with no help, but God said, "I know." He went on to say in Genesis 16:11 that she would have a son and that they would be all right, "because the Lord has given heed to your affliction."

Now notice Genesis 16:13: "Then she called the name of the Lord who spoke to her, 'You are a God who sees.'" The Hebrew word for the name Hagar gave to God is *El Roi*. *El Roi* simply means that God sees. Do you know that God sees? He sees the circumstances you're in. He sees you out there in the desert all alone with no one to provide for you, give you spiritual and emotional covering, and protect you. He is not unaware of what you're going through. No matter what your family situation may be, no matter what your need or loss, God says, "I see. I hear. I know."

Genesis 16:15 records the birth of Ishmael and his naming by Abram, under God's direction. Now every time Abram called Ishmael by name, he, too, would be reminded of the trouble he had made. He would remember, "God knows the situation I have created."

The angel of the Lord showed up in a bad situation, but the saga of Hagar does not end here. Turn to Genesis 21, and look at the conclusion of the story. Hagar had gone back to Sarah, as the Lord told her to do. And by now Sarah had borne Isaac, the son of promise whom she and Abraham (their names were changed in chapter 17) were waiting for all along.

Both mothers and their sons were living in the same tent. And there was trouble. Sarah saw Ishmael making fun of Isaac, the son of promise (Genesis 21:9). She didn't like that at all. Ishmael was a teenager now. Teenagers will do that. But Sarah said, "Not in my house you won't!"

Abraham didn't like this mess any better than he did the first one, but Sarah demanded he give Hagar her marching papers. Abraham was very distressed, but God assured him that He was in control and that He would personally care for Hagar and Ishmael (Genesis 21:12-13). So, according to verse 14, Abraham sent Hagar and Ishmael away from his house to wander in the wilderness alone. Hagar was now a bona fide single mother.

Soon the water Abraham gave to her and the boy was used up, and she left him so she wouldn't have to watch him die (Genesis 21:15-16). But the angel of God showed up again, assuring Hagar that God knew exactly what was happening and would not only keep her and Ishmael alive, but would also make a great nation out of him (verses 17-18).

This is a classic single-parent scenario—one that, with a few changes of detail and geography, could easily be repeated today. Hagar lost her home, she had a teenage son to take care of, and she was on the streets, so to speak, with no money in her pockets. She was thirsty and probably hungry. She feared that her son would die. So, in despair, she sat down and cried.

That's when the Son of God showed up in His Old Testament form. He asked Hagar, "What is the matter with you?" (Genesis 21:17). Didn't He know the mess she was in? Of course He did. He was saying, "Hagar, have you forgotten what I did for you earlier? Have you forgotten how I found you out in the wilderness when you were pregnant and Sarah had chased you away? Do you think I'm going to remember you one minute and forget you the next? You yourself said I am the God who sees. Do you think that now I've gone blind?"

Single parent, God has not gone blind. He sees, He hears, and He knows. You may be in a far-from-ideal situation, but you have an ideal

God. You have got a God who, when your husband and the father of your baby forces you out of the home, will turn into a husband, if necessary, and be a Father to your child or children. God will always provide.

Why? Because His name is El Roi, "the God who sees." He is the way out of your lonely and negative circumstances. Now, I can't promise He will bring you a mate or a home or anything on your wish list. But I can tell you that He sees you and your child or children, and He hears your cry. He says, "Remember, I named Ishmael. And any child who has My name, I am going to take care of."

Genesis 21:18-21, the final chapter of this biblical saga, shows how God fulfilled His word. The well Hagar saw in verse 19 was there all the time, but she was so consumed with sadness and crying and forgetting God that she had stopped trusting; she had stopped looking for God.

The God Who Provides

How many times has God opened your eyes and shown you a well, a source of supply, when you didn't see any way, with no husband, that you would be able to make it? How many times has God opened your eyes and shown you how you can make it on one person's salary alone?

A sister in our church who is a single parent once came to see me. Her whole world had collapsed. Her boss had asked her to do something on her job that was against the law and against her moral code as a Christian. She refused to do it, but he told her that if she didn't, he would fire her. She said she just did not see a way to keep her job, so we called on God together.

I got a call two days later. "Let me tell you what Jesus did," she began, and she went on to tell me how Jesus had made a way. Sometime after the boss had told her he would fire her, he was found out and fired instead. She was then promoted to his position. I wasn't surprised. God knows where you are. He is the God who sees you.

The greatest thing a single parent can do is to have a passion for God, because when you have a passion for God, you have Someone who can be a Father to your child and a Husband, a protector, to you. This is a divine benefit available to all single parents who agree to function as kingdom singles who fully and freely live all of life under the lordship of Jesus Christ and who raise their children to do the same.

Single mothers should also expose their children to quality Christian men in the church so their boys grow up seeing examples of godly manhood and their daughters witness what a true kingdom single man looks like.

God will cover and surround you with either His own direct care or the care of others when you, as a single parent, whether male or female, look to Him.

∽o∾

How many times has God opened your eyes and shown you a well, a source of supply, when you didn't see any way that you would be able to make it?

∽o∾

This was brought home forcefully in my own home a long time ago when my daughter Chrystal was not yet married. Chrystal's life revolves around a schedule notebook she carries. She keeps all her plans, papers, credit cards, and many other important things in this notebook. One day she inadvertently put it on top of her car and then drove off, forgetting it was on the roof. She got home and discovered it was gone. She remembered what she had done and drove back over to the mall to look for it. But her notebook was nowhere to be found. She came back home crying.

As she sat there shedding tears, she began flipping through her daily calendar. She came to one of the verses and read this statement under it: "God will be a husband to you if you need one."

Chrystal looked at that statement and prayed, "God, You said You would be a husband to someone who needs one. I need You to be a husband to me right now and find this book that has my life in it."

When she had said that, the telephone rang. A man asked, "Is this Chrystal Evans?" She said it was. He explained that he had been driving down the street when he saw something that looked like a book lying alongside the road. He thought it looked important, so he doubled back and picked it up.

He brought it home and saw Chrystal's name in it. "I live fifty miles from there," he went on. "I just happened to be in that neighborhood today. I wanted to know if I can bring you your notebook tomorrow morning."

I want you to know we had church in the Evans house that night! We had church because even though Chrystal did not know where her notebook was, El Roi, "the God who sees," knew where it was. He came through at just the right time. I went with her to pick up the notebook and meet the man. He said, "By the way, I'm a Christian." God can make a way where there seems to be no way. God says He will never leave you by yourself.

Now, I know someone will say that was luck. Others will say it happened just by chance. But there is going to come a day when you will lose more than a notebook, and on that day you'll need to know who Jesus is. He is the angel of the Lord, "the God who sees." That's the message here. If you're not in an ideal situation, God is here to make up the difference. Hagar, don't just sit there crying. Call on the name of the Lord. He will hear you.

CONCLUSION

My wife, Lois, is an awesome cook. When our kids were growing up, she would fix huge Sunday meals. These would be composed of a roast, potatoes, green beans, corn bread, iced tea, and topped off with a 7UP cake and ice cream. I couldn't wait to get home after preaching in order to dive into the delicious meal.

But even though Lois would cook for Sunday, she wasn't about to do this again on Monday. On Monday, she became the Tupperware Queen. On Monday, she gathered everything left over from Sunday that had been stored in those Tupperware containers in the fridge, then reconfigured it all to make something brand-new.

One time I watched Lois take a casserole dish from the cabinet and then start putting the leftovers from Sunday into it. First, she would dice them and chop them to get them just right. Then she would sprinkle them into the casserole dish, layering them on top of each other. After that, she would grate some cheese and place it on top. The final ingredient would be a couple of cans of cream of mushroom soup.

Lois then stuck the dish in the oven, heated it up, and served it to all of us for dinner. Now, I know that these were just leftovers. But that was some of the best food I have ever eaten. Why? Because they were leftovers in the hands of a master.

Friend, I don't know how you have arrived at reading this book on singleness. Perhaps you've arrived with a slew of mistakes, or even a pile of successes. But whatever the case, God is able to take all your yesterdays—chop them, season them, mix them, and then sprinkle a little Holy Ghost over them—and serve you up a future that will blow your mind. He is the consummate Master, and He desires to do just that.

God longs for you to be a kingdom single by coming under His rule first. If you will simply obey God and align yourself beneath Him in all areas of your life, you can then watch how He can take what's left and turn it into something amazing. Scripture is full of people who saw big turnarounds, whether it was Rahab, Sarah, Peter, Esther, Moses, David, Solomon, Hannah, or one of many more. The Bible is full of those individuals who may have felt like giving up, but when they pushed through in faith, they saw God hit a bull's-eye with a crooked stick.

> *If you will simply obey God and align yourself beneath Him in all areas of your life, you can then watch how He can take what's left and turn it into something amazing.*

So my encouragement to you is to hang in there as you come under this kingdom rule of God. And then sit back and watch Him blow your mind as His special kingdom single.

APPENDIX:
SINGLES AND SAME-SEX ATTRACTION

One of the growing challenges facing Christian singles today is the issue of same-sex attraction. With the ever-escalating cultural and institutional acceptance, advertisement, promotion, and endorsement of homosexuality and same-sex relationships, coupled with the devaluing of biblical marriage and the lack of available mates (especially for women), same-sex attraction has become mainstream and is becoming more accepted among professing Christian singles. Add to that the increase in physical and sexual abuse, parental neglect in families, along with the inbred evil desires of our unredeemed humanity (the flesh—Romans 7:14-25), and we see that the personal, social, and cultural table has been amply set for the proliferation of the struggle and temptation of same-sex attraction, as well as its accompanying sins on both an emotional and physical level.

There are two extremes among Christians in dealing with this issue. One is to accept same-sex attraction as natural, God-given, and a matter of personal preference. The other is to treat it as though it's the only moral sin (because God condemns all sexual relationships outside of heterosexual marriage; Hebrews 13:4). This attitude leads to people who struggle with same-sex attraction being shunned, stigmatized, and condemned without compassion. However, biblical balance is possible. Compassion can exist without compromise.

Scripture is abundantly clear that homosexuality (i.e., sexual intimacy between people of the same gender, not just feelings of physical attraction and/or emotional connectedness) is not only a sin (Genesis 19:1-9; Leviticus 18:22; 20:13; 1 Timothy 1:8-11), but also a sin contrary to nature (Romans 1:26-27), since God's creation intent is for sexual relationships to exist only between a man and a woman in the context of marriage (Genesis 2:22-25; Matthew 19:4-6). Scripture is also clear that acceptance and cultivation of the illegitimate feelings (unnatural affections—Colossians 3:5; 2 Timothy 3:3; 1 Corinthians 6:9) that drive people to "act out" immorally is also sin.

∽∘∾

Compassion can exist without compromise.

∽∘∾

Yet feelings of same-sex attraction are very real and just don't disappear on their own, especially when the flesh (the desire to please self independently of God) has created an addiction to the desire. Thus this issue of same-sex attraction, for Christian singles, must be addressed with compassion without compromise. In such cases, Scripture clearly exhorts us to lovingly and patiently work with sincere believers caught in a sin who desire spiritual victory in their lives (Galatians 6:1-2; 1 Thessalonians 5:14).

How, then, should serious Christian singles deal with their struggle with same-sex attraction? First and foremost, they must resist the temptation to justify their feelings just because they're real. They must believe and speak what God says about the issue (Isaiah 5:20). They must also practice saying to themselves what God says about them in spite of how they feel. God says His children are blood bought, forgiven men and women of God who should define themselves by their relationship to Christ, not their struggles with identity, emotions, physical attraction, or sexual temptation (Galatians 2:20). While these struggles are real and not to be ignored, they are not to define who we are. God will not deliver us when we compromise with or accept the unrighteous values, perspectives, and beliefs of this world system (Romans 12:3; 1 John 2:15-17; James 1:5; 4:4-8).

Second, they must prioritize holiness (Ephesians 4:24; 1 Thessalonians 4:7), which means setting their sexuality apart to God's glory over their physical desires, just as a single Christian must do who is sinfully attracted to a person of the opposite sex. Pleasing God must trump pleasing ourselves (1 Corinthians 6:19-20; 2 Timothy 2:4; 2 Corinthians 5:9).

Third, they must practice walking in the Spirit, which involves sharing Christ's mind on every matter (2 Corinthians 10:5) and calling on the Lord and quoting His powerful Word every time they are tempted (Matthew 4:1-11; Ephesians 6:17). Then they must depend on the Holy Spirit to override the sinful desire of their flesh and take specific steps of obedience to accompany prayer and their use of the Word. God promises that when this is done, He will give believers the power to not yield to the desires of the flesh. Please note that the promise is not that the desire will disappear, but that it will not be fulfilled or acted upon (Galatians 5:16-17).

Fourth, they must connect with a solid church family that has a biblical and lovingly compassionate environment of acceptance of, and ministry to, people righteously struggling with same-sex attraction. A healthy spiritual community should be a place where it's safe to be vulnerable and take off the mask. Becoming an active part of the right spiritual family also provides the opportunity to minister to others, which is a critical tool God uses to keep us from a self-centered focus, as well as for returning to us the blessings and help we have given others (Luke 6:38; Hebrews 10:24-25; Acts 20:35; Proverbs 11:25).

God will use all these practices to give sincere Christian singles kingdom authority to progress through the temptations of same-sex attraction (1 Corinthians 10:13), so that they are controlling their fleshly desires and are not being controlled by them (Romans 8:1-13).

∞∞

Focus on and prioritize your pursuit of holiness.

∞∞

If you're struggling with same-sex attraction, don't focus on trying to move from feelings of being gay to becoming straight, but rather focus on and prioritize your pursuit of holiness. Whether or not you develop a desire for or establish a relationship with someone of the opposite sex, you can still experience the transformational work of God in your life. Your pursuit of holiness will make it possible for you to know and experience God's presence and power (Hebrews 12:14). Remember, God's grace is much greater than our sin (Romans 5:20), and that same grace enables us to deal victoriously with our struggles and weaknesses (Hebrews 4:14-16).

For more information or help on this subject, call the Focus on the Family counseling line at 855-771-4357.

ACKNOWLEDGMENTS

My deepest thanks go to Heather Hair for her skills and insights in collaboration on this book and the entire Kingdom line of books. I also want to express my heartfelt gratitude to Focus on the Family and Tyndale House Publishers for the support, commitment, and excellence they have given to this work.

NOTES

Chapter 2

1. To read more on the kingdom agenda, see Tony Evans, *The Kingdom Agenda: Life under God* (Chicago: Moody Publishers, 2013).

Chapter 12

1. Anita Chandra, Steven C. Martino, Rebecca L. Collins, Marc N. Elliott, Sandra H. Berry, David E. Kanouse, Angela Miu, "Does Watching Sex on Television Predict Teen Pregnancy? Findings from a National Longitudinal Survey of Youth," *Pediatrics* 122, no. 5 (November 2008), 1047-1054. http://pediatrics.aappublications .org/content/122/5/1047.

2. James Strong, *Strong's Exhaustive Concordance of the Bible* (Peabody, MA: Hendrickson Publishers, 2009), H3405.

3. Strong, G4203.

4. Strong, H7901.

5. Strong, G2853.

Tony EVANS
THE URBAN ALTERNATIVE

YOUR *Eternity* IS OUR *Priority*

At The Urban Alternative, eternity is our priority—for the individual, the family, the church and the nation. The 45-year teaching ministry of Tony Evans has allowed us to reach a world in need with:

The Alternative – Our flagship radio program brings hope and comfort to an audience of millions on over 1,400 radio outlets across the country.

tonyevans.org – Our library of teaching resources provides solid Bible teaching through the inspirational books and sermons of Tony Evans.

Tony Evans Training Center – Experience the adventure of God's Word with our online classroom, providing at-your-own-pace courses for your PC or mobile device.

Tony Evans app – Packed with audio and video clips, devotionals, Scripture readings and dozens of other tools, the mobile app provides inspiration on-the-go.

**Explore God's kingdom today.
Live for more than the moment.
Live for *eternity*.**

tonyevans.org

THE KINGDOM SERIES
FROM DR. TONY EVANS

MORE RESOURCES TO GROW YOUR FAITH AND FURTHER GOD'S KINGDOM!

KINGDOM MAN
978-1-58997-685-6

KINGDOM MAN
DEVOTIONAL
978-1-62405-121-0

KINGDOM WOMAN
978-1-58997-743-3

KINGDOM WOMAN
DEVOTIONAL
978-1-62405-122-7

KINGDOM WOMAN
VIDEO STUDY
978-1-62405-209-5

KINGDOM MARRIAGE
978-1-58997-820-1

KINGDOM MARRIAGE
DEVOTIONAL
978-1-58997-856-0

KINGDOM MARRIAGE
VIDEO STUDY
978-1-58997-834-8

RAISING KINGDOM KIDS
978-1-58997-784-6

RAISING KINGDOM KIDS
DEVOTIONAL
978-1-62405-409-9

RAISING KINGDOM KIDS
VIDEO STUDY
978-1-62405-407-5

KINGDOM FAMILY
DEVOTIONAL
978-1-58997-855-3

CP0845

FOCUS ON THE FAMILY®

Welcome to the Family

Whether you purchased this book, borrowed it, or received it as a gift, thanks for reading it! This is just one of many insightful, biblically based resources that Focus on the Family produces for people in all stages of life.

Focus is a global Christian ministry dedicated to helping families thrive as they celebrate and cultivate God's design for marriage and experience the adventure of parenthood. Our outreach exists to support individuals and families in the joys and challenges they face, and to equip and empower them to be the best they can be.

Through our many media outlets, we offer help and hope, promote moral values and share the life-changing message of Jesus Christ with people around the world.

Focus on the Family MAGAZINES

These faith-building, character-developing publications address the interests, issues, concerns, and challenges faced by every member of your family from preschool through the senior years.

For More INFORMATION

 ONLINE:
Log on to
FocusOnTheFamily.com/magazines
In Canada, log on to
FocusOnTheFamily.ca

PHONE:
Call toll-free:
**800-A-FAMILY
(232-6459)**
In Canada, call toll-free:
800-661-9800

FOCUS ON THE FAMILY®	FOCUS ON THE FAMILY CLUBHOUSE®	FOCUS ON THE FAMILY CLUBHOUSE JR.®	FOCUS ON THE FAMILY BRIO™	FOCUS ON THE FAMILY CITIZEN®
Marriage & Parenting	Ages 8 to 12	Ages 3 to 7	Teen Girls	U.S. News Issues

CP0552
Rev. 6/17